Aleksandr Solzhenitsyn

THE MAJOR NOVELS

Aleksandr Solzhenitsyn

THE MAJOR NOVELS

by Abraham Rothberg

Cornell University Press · Ithaca and London

Quotations from *One Day in the Life of Ivan Denisovich*, by Alexander Solzhenitsyn, English translation copyright © 1963 by E. P. Dutton & Co., Inc., New York, and Victor Gollancz Ltd, London, published by E. P. Dutton & Co., Inc., are reprinted by permission of E. P. Dutton, Inc., and Victor Gollancz Ltd. Quotations from *My Testimony*, by Anatoly Marchenko, copyright © 1969 by Anatoly Marchenko in original Russian, English translation copyright © 1969 by Michael Scammell, published by E. P. Dutton, Inc., and by Pall Mall Press, are reprinted by permission.

Quotations from *Cancer Ward*, by Alexander Solzhenitsyn, translated by Nicholas Bethell and David Burg, are by permission of Farrar, Straus & Giroux, Inc., and The Bodley Head Ltd, © The Bodley Head, 1968, 1969; quotations from pages 539 to 560 of the American edition © Farrar, Straus & Giroux, Inc., 1960.

Quotations from *The First Circle*, by Aleksandr Solzhenitsyn, translated from the Russian by Thomas P. Whitney, English translation copyright © 1968 by Harper & Row, Publishers, Inc., are reprinted by permission of Harper & Row, Publishers, Inc., and William Collins Sons & Co. Ltd. Quotations from *Will the Soviet Union Survive until 1984?* (1970), by Andrei Amalrik, are by permission of Harper & Row, Publishers, Inc.

Acknowledgment is made also to the editors of *Southwest Review* and *Interplay*, where portions of this book appeared in somewhat different form.

International Standard Book Number 0-8014-0668-4
Library of Congress Catalog Card Number 70-164641

Printed in the United States of America by Vail-Ballou Press, Inc.

For

RALPH COHEN

scholar, critic, friend

Contents

↑ Preface

Some human experiences are so traumatic that they leave forever their mark on those who have endured them—and survived. Most people who have undergone such experiences try to forget them as swiftly as possible, try to bury them beyond the furthest reaches of recollection and even of dreams; but others, a small number, are not only compelled to recall the events, but thereafter to bear witness, to give testimony, to tell the world what they were like. So it has been and still is with the survivors of Hitler's holocaust; so, too, with those who have lived through the whirlwind of Stalinism. Slowly but surely, purposely and accidentally, legally and illegally, works bearing witness are coming out of the Soviet Union, and they have been coming out in greater numbers since the death of Stalin. Some of these Russian writings are nonfiction, some fiction, but none has received more attention than the work of Aleksandr Solzhenitsyn.

In the years since the publication of *One Day in the Life*

of Ivan Denisovich, the man and his writings have come
to enjoy a singular importance in the Soviet Union, an
importance beyond that of any other contemporary writer,
and a position and influence comparable only to Gorky's in
his time, though of a very different sort. The reasons for
the acclaim and the opprobrium, the respect and the
denigration accorded to Solzhenitsyn are complicated, but
the single overriding reason is that he has chosen to write
honestly about present-day Soviet life. He has subjected
the circles within circles of that society to an old-fashioned
and refreshingly scrupulous moral scrutiny which refuses
to accept ideological cant and hypocrisy, which continually
connects ends and means, which stresses the almost un-
bridgeable gulf between the words and the deeds, the
promises and the achievements of the Soviet state. For
Russia and its peoples, Solzhenitsyn has a consuming love
which still sees his native land suffering and exploited,
martyred and mismanaged by its own rulers. His viewpoint
is so clearly rooted in personal experience with the country and its peoples that neither his sincerity nor the truth-
fulness of his observation can be called into serious question.

If Solzhenitsyn has chosen and been compelled to bear
witness for the individual Russian citizen and the whole of
Soviet society, flayed as they have been by the whirlwind
events of the past four decades, he does so as one who has
felt many of those stripes on his own flesh—and is feeling
them still. The complex interweaving of what Solzhenitsyn
the man has endured, what Solzhenitsyn the artist has por-

trayed, and what Solzhenitsyn the public figure stands for has given his work a special and undeniable force. It has conferred on him the aura of prophet, saint, and martyr with which Russians traditionally have sought to surround their literary heroes. Because his own life is in great measure representative of the experience of his whole generation, because his writing is so profoundly and intimately rooted in that experience, because he has refused to be destroyed or cowed into submission by that experience and has insisted on writing truthfully about it and publicly defending the truths of his life and the ideals of his heart, his life and work are more than a mere paradigm to his people. Instead, both have come to be looked on as a symbol: the expression of the conscience of Russia. As a result, Solzhenitsyn has been able to make literary, political, and ethical waves in Soviet life such as very few Soviet writers could make, and which, under present-day circumstances, even fewer would care to make.

ABRAHAM ROTHBERG

New York, New York

⭡ Aleksandr Solzhenitsyn:
⭡ Chronology

December 11, 1918	Born in Kislovodsk, in the Caucasus.
1938	Enters the University of Rostov-on-Don as a student of mathematics and physics.
1940	Marries fellow student Natalya Reshetovskaya.
1941	Graduates from the University of Rostov.
1942–1945	An artillery officer in the Red Army during World War II; twice decorated for valor.
February 1945	Arrested by Soviet counterintelligence for slandering Stalin in personal letters to a friend.
July 1945	Sentenced to eight years by a three-man military tribunal, one of the notorious "troikas." Sent to a labor camp.
1946–1949?	A mathematician in a prison research institute, Mavrino, on the outskirts of Moscow.

1950–1953	In a Kazakhstan concentration camp; divorced by his wife; undergoes an early cancer operation in the camp.
1953–1954	Completes his concentration-camp sentence but is forced to remain in "perpetual" exile in Kazakhstan; begins to write. The cancer recurs; goes to hospital in Tashkent, in Uzbekistan, where modern x-ray and hormone treatments arrest the cancer.
1957	Rehabilitated in the post-Stalin rehabilitations; returns to Russia, to Ryazan, where he teaches mathematics in a ten-year school.
November 1962	*One Day in the Life of Ivan Denisovich* is published in *Novy mir*, with Khrushchev's express approval, after Khrushchev has overridden objections in the Politburo.
January and July 1963	*Novy mir* publishes three Solzhenitsyn short stories: "Matryona's House," "The Incident at Krechetovka Station," and "For the Good of the Cause."
December 1963–April 1964	Debate about awarding the Lenin Prize to Solzhenitsyn for *Ivan Denisovich;* in April, a *Pravda* editorial announces that the Party has ruled against Solzhenitsyn's receiving the prize.
Late 1964	*The First Circle* is completed; the

manuscript and other private papers are confiscated by the secret police.

Early 1965   Protests against the seizure of his papers and manuscripts.

May 16, 1967   Writes a letter to the Fourth Congress of Soviet Writers condemning official censorship of belles-lettres and calls for the Writers' Union to defend and protect writers instead of acting as a repressive arm of the government.

June 12, 1967   Unpublicized meeting with the heads of the Writers' Union to discuss his demands; no results.

September 12, 1967   Writes a second letter, to the Writers' Union, objecting to the suppression of his letter to the Fourth Congress of Writers and to the government campaign of slander and harassment against him.

September 22, 1967   Meets the Board of the Writers' Union; the Board insists that he renounce "his role as leader of the political opposition" in the Soviet Union and dissociate himself from the "anti-Soviet" propaganda in the West being "carried on in his name." He refuses.

December 1, 1967   Puts eight questions in writing to the Secretariat of the Writers' Union, asking the Union to defend him against the three-year-old campaign of slander and harassment and to see that his works are published.

April 11, 1968	The *London Times Literary Supplement* prints excerpts from *Cancer Ward*.
April 18, 1968	Writes a letter to the newspapers denouncing the peddling of his manuscripts abroad by the Soviet secret police.
April 21, 1968	Writes a letter to *Literaturnaya gazeta* denying foreign publishers authorization to publish his novels.
May 1968	Circulates an open letter to the entire membership of the Writers' Union noting that, though a year has passed, no answers to his questions have been forthcoming, nor have changes in his own status or that of his books.
September 1968	*The First Circle* is published in English.
October 1968	*Cancer Ward* is published in English.
March 1969	Rumors that a sequel to *The First Circle*, called *Archipelago Gulag*, has been smuggled out to the West without the author's consent or knowledge.
August 14, 1969	Rolf Hochhuth writes an open letter to President Nikolai Podgorny protesting Solzhenitsyn's status and the banning of his books; the letter is also signed by Heinrich Böll, Arthur Miller, Martin Niemöller, and Giangiacomo Feltrinelli.
November 4, 1969	Expelled from the local branch of the Writers' Union in Ryazan; the expul-

sion is confirmed in Moscow eight days later.

| November 27, 1969 | Writes a letter of protest to the RSFSR Writers' Union condemning his ouster, the way it was conducted, and the Union's attitude toward writers. |

November 30, 1969   *Literaturnaya gazeta* suggests that he be given an exit visa and allowed to emigrate.

December 1969   Western writers and cultural organizations protest his dismissal from the Writers' Union.

December 30, 1969   Twenty-nine Soviet dissidents publicly protest his expulsion from the Writers' Union.

March 11, 1970   Appoints Zurich attorney Fritz Heeb to protect his copyrights and general interests as an author in foreign countries.

June 16, 1970   Publicly denounces the government's detention of Zhores Medvedev in a psychiatric hospital.

October 9, 1970   Awarded the Nobel Prize for literature; says he will go to Stockholm to accept the prize personally if permitted; the Soviet press launches a campaign against his receiving the award and accuses him of presenting a distorted picture of Soviet life and contributing to "anti-Soviet" propaganda and agitation.

October 11, 1970 — Thirty-seven Soviet dissidents, led by Pyotr Yakir and Zinaida Grigorenko, applaud the award of the Nobel Prize to Solzhenitsyn.

October 1970 — Cellist Mstislav Rostropovich writes a letter to leading Soviet newspapers defending Solzhenitsyn, applauding his receiving the Nobel Prize, and defending his criticisms of censorship; the letter is not published in the USSR, but Rostropovich is forbidden to travel abroad on a concert tour.

November 27, 1970 — Announces that he will not go to Stockholm to receive the Nobel Prize for literature.

December 10, 1970 — The Swedish Academy awards the Nobel Prize for literature to Solzhenitsyn *in absentia;* announcement is made in Moscow that he has joined the Committee for Human Rights, established in November by physicists Andrei Sakharov, Andrei Tverdokhlebov, and Valery Chalidze.

June 1971 — Allows his new novel, *August 1914,* the first volume in a fictional trilogy devoted to Russia's role in World War I, to be published in Russian by a small press in Paris. Gives as his reason the fact that it could not be published in the Soviet Union.

Aleksandr Solzhenitsyn

THE MAJOR NOVELS

I bow down before the might of the human Spirit. I find the thought offensive that all of [man's] most majestic creations are no more than mold growing on a rock, the name of which is Economics. Even admitting that what I call Spirit is nothing but matter that has become conscious of itself, I still know that man, having learned to think, *ipso facto* revolted against the yoke of his material nature and will rather destroy himself than renounce the spiritual values that have be... revealed to him.

Aleksandr Kron

1 ⁑ The Writer's Life

A hard life improves the vision.

Aleksandr Solzhenitsyn

In an era when daily events continue to outstrip even the wildest fantasies, and when movies and television allow their audiences immediate apprehensions of experience, readers have come to require of fiction an increasing degree of intimate knowledge of reality and verisimilitude in its portrayal. Writers have, consequently, been faced with greater and greater difficulties in writing realistic, believable novels rooted in life. Since most novelists have usually written out of their own knowing and feeling—autobiographically, if you will, but in the very broadest sense—they have "sought experience" in their lives to employ in their fictions. Solzhenitsyn has had no need to seek out experience: it has come to him.

Though the facts of his life available to Westerners are sparse and, for a variety of reasons, no comprehensive biographical data have been released in the Soviet Union,[1] some contradictory but illuminating material can be gleaned. Aleksandr Isaevich Solzhenitsyn was born on December 11, 1918, the descendant of Cossack intellectuals, in the small resort town of Kislovodsk, in the Caucasus. Before he was born, his father was killed in a hunting accident, and Aleksandr was brought up by his mother, who worked as a typist, in Rostov-on-Don, six hundred miles south of Moscow. In 1941, a few days before the war between Nazi Germany and the Soviet Union began, he was graduated from the University of Rostov with a degree in physics and mathematics. Solzhenitsyn has himself testi-

[1] Soviet authorities seem deliberately to have suppressed the facts of Solzhenitsyn's life and career in order to raise doubts about his character, imprisonment, and war record. The novelist, on the other hand, because of his precarious relations with the authorities, has been wary of granting interviews to foreign reporters—an understandable precaution, in Soviet circumstances, against giving even the impression of being "connected" to the West or caring about its opinions or applause. As late as 1970, when one of Solzhenitsyn's English translators, Nicholas Bethell, was in the USSR and asked to see him, Solzhenitsyn was not granting interviews. Bethell wrote: "He has never been interviewed by a Westerner and now is not the time to begin" (*New York Times Magazine*, April 12, 1970, p. 6). Solzhenitsyn, however, did grant an interview to the Czechoslovak, Russian-speaking Pavel Licko three years earlier. The interview, entitled "One Day with Alexander Isaevich Solzhenitsyn," was printed on March 31, 1967, in the Slovak journal *Kulturny Zivot*, a paper which was one of the press leaders in the liberalization in Czechoslovakia. The interview appeared, in excerpts, in English in *Soviet Survey*, July 1967, under the title "One Day with Solzhenitsyn—An Interview." Even Licko had great difficulty in interviewing Solzhenitsyn, though the bar-

fied: "I was not sure what to do next. I was good at mathematics and it was suggested that I should do postgraduate work, research. I never intended to devote myself to mathematics. Literature was the greatest attraction, but I realized that mathematics would at least provide me with bread and butter." As a result Solzhenitsyn "made no special study of literature until he was twenty-one and took a correspondence course at the Philological Department of Moscow University."[2] For a time he was stage-struck, but after he had failed his acting tryouts, and been afflicted with laryngitis, his interest turned to playwriting.

At the university, Solzhenitsyn had met Natalya Reshetovskaya, a science student who was studying to be a

---

riers raised were chiefly those of the regime. In *Svetova Literatura* (No. 4, July 1968), Licko tells how from 1966 onward he had requested permission to interview Solzhenitsyn from "the comrade in charge of the section of the Soviet Writers' Union responsible for this sort of thing"—but in vain. He was told that the novelist was so gravely ill that he could not receive visitors. Finally, Licko wrote directly to Solzhenitsyn and by return mail was invited to visit him. Solzhenitsyn told Licko why he had declined the invitation of the Czechoslovak Writers' Union to visit Czechoslovakia, and it is indicative of the role the Soviet Writers' Union plays with respect to Soviet writers. The invitation of Solzhenitsyn came from the Czechoslovak Writers' Union to the Soviet Union, and the Soviet Union wrote to Solzhenitsyn: "The Czechoslovak Writers' Union has invited you to visit Czechoslovakia. Reply through us that you cannot accept due to illness."

[2] Licko, p. 182. The interview reports that Solzhenitsyn was graduated from the University of Moscow, but all other sources disagree. Licko may have mistaken this correspondence course for Solzhenitsyn's other education and so confused Moscow University with the University of Rostov.

teacher, and he married her in 1940. Not long afterward, the Germans invaded Russia, and directly after graduation, Solzhenitsyn joined the Red Army. He was sent to artillery school, where he finished the training course for junior officers and then was dispatched on a two-week journey to the Gorki region. "All I saw and experienced [here]," he said, "is reflected in *An Incident at Krechetovka Station*." Subsequently shipped to the front as an artillery officer, he saw heavy combat, was eventually promoted to captain in charge of a battery in the Leningrad sector, and twice decorated.[3] In February 1945, during the battle of Königsberg, in East Prussia, he was stripped of his badge of rank and decorations, and his revolver confiscated by his divisional commander: he was put under arrest. As Solzhenitsyn describes it, "For a long time I had been sending a friend letters clearly criticising Stalin without mentioning his name. I thought he had betrayed Leninism and was responsible for the defeats in the first phase of the war, that he was a weak theoretician, and that his language was primitive." [4] Indiscreetly, Solzhenitsyn and his friend continued to make such comments in their letters, superficially disguising their references to the dictator by alluding to him as "the whiskered one," *khozyain* ("master"), or *balabos* (Yiddish for

[3] *Ibid.* This is an additional and obvious error. Licko writes that Solzhenitsyn "marched from Orel through White Russia to Berlin," and then goes on to say that the novelist was arrested in January 1945 during the battle of Königsberg.
[4] *Ibid.*

"boss").[5] Not surprisingly, Russian counterintelligence [6] was reading military mail, and that same month its agents picked up Solzhenitsyn, interrogated and beat him, then transported him to the infamous Lubyanka Prison in Moscow, where he was held.

Without a hearing, one of Stalin's notorious three-man summary courts, the so-called troikas, sentenced Solzhenitsyn to eight years in prison and perpetual exile thereafter. (In an exchange with Konstantin Fedin at a session of the Board of the Union of Soviet Writers in 1967, Solzhenitsyn remarked bitterly: "An individual who now occupies a very high office publicly stated that he is sorry he was not one of the *troika* that sentenced me in 1945, that he would have sentenced me to be shot then and there!" The man in question was identified as Alexei Romanov, now chairman of the State Cinematography Committee, and it was evidently he who denounced Solzhenitsyn in 1945.) [7]

The new prisoner was at first assigned to laying parquet flooring in a Moscow apartment house being built for

[5] *Balabos* is a corruption of the Hebrew *bal habais* ("master of the house"). Svetlana Alliluyeva testifies that Stalin's entourage referred to him as *khozyain.*

[6] Smersh, an acronym for the Russian words "Death to Spies!"

[7] Much biographical information on the novelist appeared in an excellent critical summary of his career: "The Writer as Russia's Conscience," *Time*, Sept. 27, 1968. Earlier, in winter 1962, and only after many inquiries from foreign newsmen, the official Soviet press agency, Tass, released a single-page biography from which some facts of Solzhenitsyn's life and education could be gleaned.

secret-police officials. Solzhenitsyn later told about it thus: "I would never have survived the camp had it not been for mathematics. I was unfit for manual work and could not make moral compromises. I was employed on building sites near Moscow and in Moscow itself. On the Leninskii Prospekt there is a large building with turrets and a shop called Spartak on the ground floor. I worked there." [8] Because he filled out a questionnaire which told of his education in mathematics and physics, he was subsequently sent to Mavrino, a prison research institute in the Moscow suburbs,[9] "where the standard was so high that any scientist would have been proud to work there. As a prisoner mathematician I spent four of the eight years in good conditions." Then, evidently for having refused to cooperate with the Mavrino authorities, the secret police—"I . . . could not make moral compromises"—Solzhenitsyn was shipped to a forced-labor camp in Kazakhstan, where he became a number. "For the last three years of my sentence I was in a mining region in Kazakhstan. It was there that I conceived the idea of writing *One Day in the Life of Ivan Denisovich*. Since it was a special camp, we all had numbers stamped on the forehead, heart, knees and back. My number was Shch 232." ("A day later I went with Solzhenitsyn," the Slovak journalist Pavel Licko wrote many years

[8] Licko, p. 183. In "The Writer as Russia's Conscience," *Time* reported that, years later, "Solzhenitsyn was invited to visit a friend in that same building. He was proud to discover that his floors did not squeak."

[9] Mavrino is the setting for the novel *The First Circle*.

later, "to the elegant Lira cafe for young people in Moscow. We left our coats in the cloakroom and the attendant gave us tickets. Solzhenitsyn glanced at his cloakroom ticket and smiled: 'It seems I shall never get rid of this number.' It was 232.") [10]

After serving his eight-year term and one additional month, Solzhenitsyn was released from the camp on March 5, 1953. "I walked the streets of a town, a free but deported man. An old deaf woman woke me up one morning and forced me to go out and listen to a communique broadcast by the local radio station. Stalin's death was announced. It was my first day of freedom." [11] But Solzhenitsyn was by no means free; he was still required to live permanently in exile in Siberia: "Later on I was summoned to appear before the local committee of the security police where I was asked to sign a document confirming my permanent deportation. It was formulated exactly in this way—permanent deportation, not deportation for life. I refused to sign." [12]

Families of prisoners in the Soviet Union are subject to many kinds of discrimination, coercion, and persecution by the authorities in an endeavor to make them disown the prisoners.[13] Wives are often pressured to divorce their im-

---

[10] Licko, p. 183.

[11] *Ibid.* Solzhenitsyn commented, in the exchange with the Writers' Union board: "After having served the eight-year sentence, I was kept an additional month in prison, but it is considered shameful even to mention such a petty detail."

[12] *Ibid.*, pp. 183–184.

[13] Even with the paucity of biographical information about the novelist, one can get some feeling of these conditions by reading

prisoned husbands, and very often do so, because of the length of the sentences and the uncertainty that the men will ever be released, even after serving their sentences. While he was in prison, Solzhenitsyn persuaded his wife to divorce him. Subsequently, she remarried and had two children, but after Solzhenitsyn was released from concentration camp, Natalya divorced her second husband and rejoined Solzhenitsyn in Ryazan.[14]

In Kazakhstan he had begun to write the stories, plays, and poetry he had stored up in camp, his naturally phe-

---

the painful and moving scenes in *The First Circle* between Gleb Nerzhin and his wife. Even more painful is the powerful novel by Lydia Chukovskaya, *The Deserted House* (New York: Dutton, 1967), although there the relationship involved is between a mother and son.

[14] Though the resemblance to the love story of Dr. Zhivago and Lara in Boris Pasternak's novel, *Doctor Zhivago*, is brought painfully and forcibly to mind, Edmund Stevens, in "Solzhenitsyn Collecting the Nobel Prize," *Newark Evening News*, Nov. 4, 1970, reported from Moscow that Solzhenitsyn and his wife were now estranged. "Withal Solzhenitsyn is essentially a solitary introvert. Though he spends some of his time with wife and family in Ryazan, it is mainly from a sense of duty. The relationship could hardly be called intimate." A half year later, Bernard Gwertzman, the *New York Times* Moscow correspondent, wrote (June 19, 1971) that Solzhenitsyn had been "seeking a divorce from his wife of many years, but Mrs. Solzhenitsyn, after first saying she would consent to a divorce, was reported by his friends to have changed her mind. . . . A woman described as a mathematician in her early thirties gave birth last December to a boy, which Mr. Solzhenitysn acknowledged as his, and the boy, Yermolai A. Solzhenitsyn, was baptized. The novelist is said to want to marry the woman but is hesitant about seeking a divorce in court."

nomenal memory reinforced by having to remember everything he composed in camp, because the forced-labor-camp administration, Gulag, would give him neither paper nor writing implements. The writing came in a rush of creativity—and was stopped, once more, this time by sickness. In camp he had been crudely and ineffectively operated on for cancer; now the cancer recurred more acutely. He thereupon made his way to a hospital in Tashkent, the capital of the Uzbek SSR, where more modern and competent medical treatment succeeded in arresting the tumor.[15] "He [Solzhenitsyn] is a freak medical case: the cells of his body are not damaged by irradiation," Nicholas Bethell reported. "In 1954 this saved his life near Lake Balkhash where . . . he had to live for a time as an 'eternal exile.' The growth in his belly made it impossible for him to sleep and made him think of nothing but pain. . . . In the hospital he was given massive irradiation and injections, and in three days was a human being again. The cancer is still there, a solid lump, but it seldom bothers him and is not something his friends worry about."[16] Solzhenitsyn himself testifies that he recovered after long treatment: "The tumour does not bother me now."[17]

"In 1956," Solzhenitsyn has recounted, "I was living as a deportee on the edge of a desert to the south-west of Balkhash, in the village of Kok-Terek (Green Poplar). As a free man it would have been more difficult to find employ-

[15] The hospital in Tashkent provides the characters, locale, and experience for the novel *Cancer Ward*.
[16] Bethell, pp. 44–45.   [17] Licko, p. 184.

ment. I was in the fortunate position of being the only mathematician in the village and was easily able to find a teaching post." [18] It was not until after the Twentieth Party Congress that Solzhenitsyn (and many others like him) was rehabilitated in 1957 and permitted to return from exile. In Russia, he found a job teaching mathematics to students in a ten-year school in Ryazan; until his success as a novelist, he lived quietly in "Ryazan, a booming oil refinery city 115 miles southwest of Moscow teaching school and writing. . . . He was a well-liked teacher, a dramatic lecturer popular with his teen-age students. The Solzhenitsyn family lived in a small apartment in an old wooden building on a quiet side street and the author worked in the garden, puttered around the house, went bicycling and did some amateur photography for relaxation." [19]

Six years later, Solzhenitsyn's career as a novelist was launched with the publication of *One Day in the Life of Ivan Denisovich* in the November 1962 issue of the Soviet literary journal *Novy mir*. Few writers' careers have begun so spectacularly and the circumstances attending the publication of his first novel were unique in Russian literature. "Within a day all of the ninety-five thousand copies of the November issue of the magazine were snapped up by eager Russians. Within a week Solzhenitsyn skyrocketed to inter-

[18] *Ibid.* Solzhenitsyn also noted: "*Matryona's Home* had its origins there. The events in that story took place in 1956 and not in 1953 as was stated in the first edition."

[19] *New York Times*, June 5, 1967.

national fame." [20] Augmenting both sales and reputation was an interesting combination of political and literary circumstance whose roots go far back into the early 1920s, and even further into the depths of Russian political and literary history.

In his novels, his major works, Solzhenitsyn has set out to tear the scales from the eyes of the ordinary Russian—and it is the Russian audience which primarily concerns him—to force him to face Soviet life as it really is, shorn of ideological trappings, cant, and camouflage. This is demonstrated symbolically in Solzhenitsyn's stage setting for his play *The Love-Girl and the Innocent* in which the Potemkin façade—the bright sham disguising the drab or ugly reality—is explicit:

> The curtain rises. It is an ordinary theatre curtain, but is not used again until the end of the play. Behind it there is a second curtain—a length of fabric crudely painted with a poster-like industrial landscape, depicting cheerful, apple-cheeked, muscular men and women working away quite effortlessly. In one corner of the curtain a joyful procession is in progress complete with flowers, children and a portrait of Stalin. [21]

[20] Marvin Kalb, Introduction, *One Day in the Life of Ivan Denisovich*, trans. Ralph Parker (New York: Dutton, 1963), p. 5.
[21] *The Love-Girl and the Innocent*, trans. Nicholas Bethell and David Burg (New York: Farrar, Straus & Giroux, 1969), unnumbered page at the beginning; quoted by permission of Farrar, Straus & Giroux, Inc., and The Bodley Head Ltd.

Beyond that curtain is a concentration camp with its prisoners and guards, its barbed wire and watchtowers. All of Solzhenitsyn's writing insists on this division between illusion and the reality and constantly peels away the Potemkin façade to depict Soviet life as a vast police-state concentration camp.

Using what at first would seem to be extreme or marginal settings and situations—a concentration camp, a prison research center, a cancer hospital—as metaphors for Soviet society, Solzhenitsyn shows them to be central to the Soviet experience, microcosms of all Soviet society. Solzhenitsyn conceives of the Soviet people as inmates of closed systems in which all are sentenced and condemned, usually unjustly and without legal recourse or appeal, and in which all are doomed. Incarcerated in penal colonies, condemned to exile, isolation, loneliness, illness, and death, all his characters are at the mercy of cruel and implacable institutions and of the vicious and violent who run them. Since the settings are places *in extremis,* there is almost no ordinary life, or else ordinary life has become so malevolent that most of its healing and solace have been lost or attenuated. There are no wives and children, no creature comforts, or very few, and his prisoners and patients remember their former, ordinary lives as unreal dreams, the daily round of common life having receded into the mists of fantasy. Thus Solzhenitsyn makes ordinary life seem extraordinary, common life uncommon, and the violations and ravages of concentration camp and police state, cancer and the cancer ward routine.

Solzhenitsyn deliberately chooses institutions which by

their nature permit the depiction of a cross section of Soviet life. People of different classes, education, and ethnic backgrounds can be shown: peasants and workers, soldiers and secret police, bureaucrats and intelligentsia are thrown together so that their varying characters and viewpoints are contrasted. Throughout there is the one constant of traditional Russian literature: the "they" of the rulers, the oppressors, and the "we" of the ruled, the oppressed, but even the rulers and oppressors are themselves ruled and oppressed by those above them in the hierarchy, so that almost all his characters are at the mercy of others, almost none have control over their own lives, almost all live in fear and servility; tyranny is epidemic and inevitable. In *Ivan Denisovich*, the "we" are the prisoners, the "they" the Gulag camp administration; in *The First Circle*, the "we" are the prisoner-scientists and technicians, the "they" their MGB (Ministry of State Security) jailers and the secret-police and government bureaucrats all the way up the hierarchy through Mikhail Ryumin and Viktor Abakumov to Stalin himself; in *Cancer Ward*, the "we" are the patients, the "they" the medical staff.

Within the institutions he portrays Solzhenitsyn shows the omnipresent pecking order, the gradations of privilege and deprivation, with everyone, or almost everyone, trying to move one or more rungs up the ladder of privilege by hook or by crook. Because almost no one is free and independence is always threatened, a meaningful mode of life, personal integrity, and a decent sense of values are always under assault, from above and from below. Even in the concentration camp there is a pecking order. At the top is the Chekist Lieutenant Volkovoi, the camp security chief, who used to beat prisoners with a "whip of plaited leather, as thick as his forearm." [22] At the very bottom, in the ranks of the prisoners, are the jackals like Fetiukov, or the "goners" (in *The Love-Girl and the Innocent*), men at the end of their tether, who search in garbage pails for food or lick out the bowls of other prisoners after they have eaten. Between the topmost and lowest levels is a whole range of meticulously graded camp authorities: officers, doctors, guards, and prisoners, criminal and political, who include foremen, trustees, warders, squad leaders, deputies, cooks, and spies.

Yet, even in the midst of human evil, weakness, illness, and corruption, there remains some core of humanity—of compassion and pleasure and even of saintliness. Most human beings settle for staying alive physically, but many try to do more, try to remain alive emotionally and intellectually, and there the heroism of common men is most apparent—as the cruelty of the system is most apparent. Some things do remain to men even in the depths: the pleasure of work and of meditation, the brief sensuous joy of the taste of bread, exercising, smoking a cigarette, staying warm or dry, the more important meanings of comradeship, the spiritual solace of religious belief or even of Communist idealism. Moreover, when men are stripped of almost everything, they are able to reacquire their integrity, able to recover their freedom, for, no longer having anything worse to fear, they can possess "the fearlessness of those who have lost

[22] *Ivan Denisovich,* p. 41.

everything"; they can speak their minds. As one of the prisoners in *The First Circle* explains to his MGB tormentor: "Just understand one thing and pass it along to anyone at the top who still doesn't know that you are strong only as long as you don't deprive people of *everything*. For a person you've taken *everything* from is no longer in your power. He's free all over again." [23]

Solzhenitsyn condemns the Soviet system absolutely, but his metaphors go beyond that country and its society to the world at large. All men in modern society are imprisoned and strait-jacketed, tormented and sick. Men are sick and so are their institutions; the jail and the cancer ward, the penal colony and the *sharashka* (a sinister enterprise based on bluff and deceit, and another form of Potemkin façade) are everywhere operative. Evil societies breed evil men, but evil men also breed evil societies; and if Solzhenitsyn refuses to damn men irretrievably, he also refuses to absolve them of responsibility. Men are responsible not only for their institutions generally but for their personal behavior specifically. Men must affirm and uphold justice, must resist and oppose injustice; morality is an obligation which men must meet, even at the cost of personal martyrdom. Ultimately, therefore, Solzhenitsyn is a moral writer, not a political one; and precisely because of that he is an even greater menace to those who now control the Soviet Union, the "heirs of Stalin." For though he is aware of men's frailties and views them with compassion, Solzhenitsyn's

[23] *The First Circle*, trans. Thomas P. Whitney (New York: Harper & Row, 1968), p. 83.

judgment of the sadists and torturers, the squealers and cheats, the slackers and parasites is severe and rigorous.

Nevertheless, the picture of Soviet life etched by Solzhenitsyn is scarcely attractive even to the most sympathetic foreign observer, much less the domestic reader who has felt on his flesh the mailed fist of Stalin and his heirs. Solzhenitsyn's fictional depiction is far more powerful and effective than the reports Western scholars, journalists, diplomats, and travelers have brought back, because he more intimately knows and more artistically renders that life; and his portrayal is far more persuasive to the Russian reader because of its unvarnished candor. Moreover, it is apparent even to the most casual or hostile reader that Solzhenitsyn has known firsthand most of what he portrays. Such knowledgeableness generally elicits audience sympathy and suspension of disbelief, and makes Solzhenitsyn a novelist all the more difficult to dismiss as wrongheaded or simply ill-informed. His obvious love for his homeland and his people, his personal and artistic insistence on ethical conduct, his almost reluctant yet proud acceptance of the mantle of moral conscience that the great Russian writers have traditionally donned, with its attendant hair shirt and crown of thorns, have lifted him above all the other contemporary writers in the Soviet Union to make him an example and a target.

> Solzhenitsyn takes for granted an absolutely direct and open connection between literature and morality, art and life. He believes our responsibilities in the one to

be inseparable from our responsibilities in the other; indeed, to be all but identical with one another.

In the West today such an assumption about the relationship between art and morality is distinctly unfashionable. We like to insist nowadays on the detachment of art from moral considerations, on the element of sheer "play" in it, on its aesthetic autonomy and aloofness from the messiness of the world in which decisions with real consequences have to be made. Or if we admit any commerce between art and morality . . . then what we are likely to demand of our art is that it should subvert and overthrow all the traditional moral notions; that it should do its best to fragment the self into a thousand pieces, rather than to stress its organic wholeness.[24]

If Solzhenitsyn has a vision of a better life, it is not a vision which he identifies with a specific social system. If he condemns Soviet society for its tyranny and evil, he does so without approving of any other form of human organization, in fact or in theory, for Solzhenitsyn is aware of how inadequate most human institutions are, how compromised and coercive. Moreover, he portrays the profound and almost ineradicable evil he sees in men, creatures full of cruelty, violence, and self-interest, of shoddiness and be-

[24] Dan Jacobson, "The Example of Solzhenitsyn," *Commentary*, May 1969, p. 82. Jacobson intelligently and perceptively reviews *The First Circle* and *Cancer Ward*. Quotations are reprinted from *Commentary* by permission; copyright © 1969 by the American Jewish Committee; copyright © Dan Jacobson.

trayals. But he also sees and depicts men's basic virtues, their comradeship and compassion, their kindness and decency, their loyalty and, in some rare instances, even their saintliness. All of Solzhenitsyn's major works are set in contexts where men have little or no control over their lives— prison, *sharashka*, cancer ward—where human beings are debased and diseased, where fear, tyranny, and pain are endemic and inevitable, but how men live under these circumstances, how they endure and remain men, is Solzhenitsyn's obsession. His characters cry out not to be shoved around. They ask to hold on to their dignity and their sovereignty. They refuse to surrender their freedom or the illusion of their freedom. To the very end they struggle to keep some corner of their minds and hearts aloof and inviolable, refusing even *in extremis* sometimes to accept direction from others, from above, even when it is, as presumably it is in *Cancer Ward*, "for their own good." If one meets an almost peasant recalcitrance here, one also finds a religious and idealistic commitment to the worth of the human individual, a refusal to consider that human being a means rather than an end, and therefore a rebelliousness against all institutions, against all the necessary and unnecessary submission to repressiveness and surrendering of sovereignty which any state—not only the totalitarian—requires of its citizens.

2 ⚴ One *Day, Four *Decades

How can you expect a man who's warm to understand a
man who's cold.

Aleksandr Solzhenitsyn

For those who experienced the Hitlerian holocaust or
the Stalinist whirlwind, there persists an obsessive desire to
record the tangible fact, the uncomplicated act, the obvious
motive, all of which serve to give the human mind a way of
hanging on to reality when the incomprehensible over-
whelms it. An understated, almost documentary recording
of the actual gives power to *One Day in the Life of Ivan
Denisovich*—and defines its limitations. The novel observes the classical unities of time, place, and action; its
events take place within a single day in January 1951 in a
Siberian concentration camp, where the 104th squad of
zeks (prisoners) builds a wall. The story is told through a
narrator, Ivan Denisovich Shukhov, now Prisoner S 854, a
Russian peasant carpenter who is serving the eighth year of
his sentence in this "special" penal colony, and through him
we are introduced to a cross section of Soviet society, individuals representing almost every class and profession and

many of the ethnic groups in the Soviet Union: police, military, peasant, worker, intellectual, Russian, Estonian, Latvian, Ukrainian, gypsy; the microcosm of this Siberian penal colony reflects the macrocosm of that greater penal colony, Russia. Among the inmates is Tiurin, a kulak's (rich peasant's) son who has spent more than twenty years in the camps; Buinovsky, a former naval captain and confirmed Communist; Tsezar, an erstwhile film producer and intellectual; Alyosha, a Baptist convicted for his religious beliefs; Volkovoi, a lieutenant in the security police and veteran Chekist; Fetiukov, a former government bureaucrat now reduced to the status of prisoner-jackal. About his intentions in the novel Solzhenitsyn was quite specific: "I have always felt that to write about the fate of Russia was the most fascinating and important task to be performed. The fate of Ivan Denisovich was the greatest tragedy in all Russian drama. While still in the camp I made up my mind to describe one day of prison life. Tolstoy once said that a novel can deal with either centuries of European history or a day in one man's life." [1] In *One Day in the Life of Ivan Denisovich*, Solzhenitsyn tried to encompass both, to present one day of the 3,653 days of Ivan Denisovich Shukhov's sentence and, simultaneously, a capsule of some four decades of Russian history.

Shukhov's day opens at five in the morning to the sound of the harsh blows of a hammer on a length of rail. Awakened, he feels sick, and is concerned that his squad may be

---

[1] "Pavel Licko, "One Day with Solzhenitsyn—An Interview," *Soviet Survey*, July 1967, p. 184.

sent that day to a new site to build a settlement on the bare
icy steppe, where for a whole month there will be no place
to get warm and where, as a consequence, many of the prisoners will die. The job of the squad leader, Tiurin, is "to
elbow some other squad, some bunch of suckers, into the assignment instead of the 104th," but for Tiurin to do that
successfully, "he'd have to take a pound of salt pork to the
senior official there [at the assignment center], if not a
couple of pounds." [2]

In opening the novel that way, Solzhenitsyn sounds a
note which he repeats in almost everything he writes: the
corruption endemic in the camps represents the corruption
of Soviet society at large, and, more, may be part and parcel
of man's nature and institutions, irrespective of the system
under which he lives. The greased palm is the order of the
day, because everyone wants some advantage or special
privilege; hence bribery, blackmail, and back-scratching
are rife: every service has a price, and almost every individual as well. Tiurin, for instance, uses salt pork to bribe
the official who assigns prisoners work and so keeps his
squad from being sent to the "Socialist Way of Life" settlement at the new site; but some other "poorer and stupider"
squad must go in its place, and its men will die on the un-
sheltered snow-covered steppe. If a man wants to get a
warm vest, he bribes someone in the "warehouse for
people's private belongings" (p. 47). Every squad is
cheated in its bread ration at the central supply depot; and

[2] *One Day in the Life of Ivan Denisovich*, trans. Ralph Parker
(New York: Dutton, 1963), pp. 19–20.

then within each squad, when the bread ration is divided among the prisoners, each individual is also shortchanged.

> [Shukhov] took a look at his ration, weighing it in his hand and hastily calculating whether it reached the regulation sixteen ounces. He had drawn many a thousand of these rations in prisons and camps, and though he'd never had an opportunity to weigh them on scales, and although, being a man of timid nature, he knew no way of standing up for his rights, he, like every other prisoner, had discovered long ago that honest weight was never to be found in the bread-cutting. There was short weight in every ration. The only point was how short. [p. 35]

In *The Love-Girl and the Innocent*, Solzhenitsyn has a scene—between the prisoner Rodion Nemov, temporarily the head of the Works and Planning Department of a concentration camp, and a woman prisoner who wants a job as a bread cutter—which shows how the system works.

> BELLA: The first thing you must do is get your own people into key positions. Otherwise you'll have no power. To be more specific, I would like to mention the matter of bread-cutting. I used to work there, but they threw me out . . . because of some *ludicrous* accusation that I was giving short measure. You can rely on me completely. If I get a job in the bread-cutting room, you will have a minimum of three kilos a day, all to yourself.
>
> NEMOV: Listen, I personally couldn't . . .

BELLA: No, it's not for you, not for you *personally*. Of course, there's no reason why *you* should eat black bread. But you can sell it. Or exchange it for vodka. Or give someone a bonus, so to speak. You see, you'll have to *pay* the people who work for you. There's no other way. [p. 40]

Food, particularly bread, means survival in the camps and therefore becomes a means of exchange, currency, what one pays off with.

Prisoners, in *Ivan Denisovich*, are permitted to receive parcels "from home," but even those zeks who do get parcels are forced into greasing palm after palm.

[The zek] has to share with the guard and the squad leader—and how can he help giving a little something to the trusty in the parcels office? Why, next time the fellow may mislay your parcel and a week may go by before your name appears again on the list! And that other fellow at the place where you hand in your food to be kept for you, safe from friskers and pilferers . . . he must have his cut too, and a good one, if you don't want him little by little swiping more than you gave him. . . . And something to the bath attendant for issuing you decent underwear—not much but something. And for the barber who shaves you "with paper" (for wiping the razor on—he usually does it on your knee). Not much to him either but, still, three or four butts. And at the C.E.D., for your letters to be kept separate and not get lost. And if you want

> to goof off a day or two and lie in bed, instead of
> going to work, you have to slip the doctor something.
> And what about the neighbor you share a locker with
> . . . ? He must have his cut. After all, he sees every
> blessed ounce you take. Who'd be nervy enough not
> to give him his share? [pp. 143–144]

Early in his sentence Shukhov had also received a few parcels from his wife, but then he wrote her: "Don't send them.
Don't take the food out of the kids' mouths" (p. 125). He
knows how very difficult it is for families on the outside
to send prisoners such parcels, knows that his family will
not be able to afford it for the ten years of his sentence, so he
has stopped his wife from even trying, yet every time Shukhov hears the call for parcels, his heart leaps with the hope
that he has been sent one. Because the authorities frown on
citizens continuing their relations with "enemies of the
people," many families stop sending prisoners parcels, and
many, like Shukhov's family, cannot afford to send them.
  The corruption carries into the work done at the camp;
vandalism, waste, and deliberate sabotage characterize the
prisoners' efforts, and stupid, inefficient cruelty those of
their jailers. Everywhere there are broken steam shovels and
dredges, burned-out motors, piles of scrap metal, and the
skeletons of half-built, abandoned buildings. Zeks are forced
to labor under conditions that cause them to use up most of
their time and effort in simply trying to make work feasible.
Shukhov and his squad, for example, are assigned to building a wall on the second story of a building, but it is so cold

that unless they can keep the men and the mortar warm, both will freeze. No provision is made by the camp authorities to keep the men warm—in fact, the authorities punish zeks who scrounge materials to protect themselves against the cold—so the men of the 104th have to steal rolls of felt to seal the open windows against the cruel wind and burn good wood in a stove Shukhov builds. Another squad is assigned to chop holes in the stone-hard frozen earth with picks, but the men are forbidden to build fires to thaw themselves or the earth; of course, they accomplish nothing; their picks simply strike sparks from the flinty ground. The greatest corruption is in the preparation of the work reports, for only by doctoring them can a squad leader keep his men alive. To get the doctored work reports approved, of course, the work inspectors' palms must be greased.

The corruption on the outside is rendered by accounts of Shukhov's thoughts about the kolkhoz (collective farm) from which he came; all the men have bribed their way out of working on the kolkhoz so that they can make money by carpet-painting. The men stencil old sheets and sell them for use as carpets, make very good profits, and leave the work of the kolkhoz to the women. For such manipulations one must be able to grease a palm, and "although Shukhov had trodden the earth for forty years, though he'd lost half his teeth and his head was growing bald, he'd never either given or taken a bribe, nor had he learned to do so in camp" (p. 50).

The basic corruption of Soviet society is reflected in the

injustices inflicted on the zeks, in the reasons and the way they were sentenced. Most of the prisoners seem to have been summarily sentenced under the catch-all Article 58 of the Criminal Code (for political crimes), sentenced indiscriminately to ten or twenty-five years. Tiurin has spent nineteen years in the camps because he concealed the fact that his father was a kulak. The former naval commander Buinovsky has been condemned to twenty-five years for spying for Britain, because he had served as a liaison officer on a British cruiser and as a token of gratitude the British admiral had after the war sent him a gift, a souvenir (p. 116). Shukhov himself has been sentenced for high treason, because in February 1942 a whole Red army had been surrounded by the Germans. Shukhov was captured, then had managed to escape and return to his own lines. There he had been accused of fabricating the escape story and been condemned for treason.

> He had testified to it himself. Yes, he'd surrendered to the Germans with the intention of betraying his country and he'd returned from captivity to carry out a mission for German intelligence. What sort of mission neither Shukhov nor the interrogator could say. So it had been left at that—a mission.
>
> Shukhov had figured it all out. If he didn't sign he'd be shot. If he signed he'd still get a chance to live. So he signed. [p. 71]

Informing, arbitrariness, and cruel punishment characterize the camps as they characterize Soviet life. Squealers "were sure to get through camp all right. Only, they were saving their own skin at the expense of other people's blood" (p. 18); even in the 104th, the prisoner Panteleyev was an informer for the security police. Volkovoi had had prisoners flogged, and "when the prisoners would be standing in a group near a barracks at the evening count, he'd slink up from behind and lash out at someone's neck with a 'Why aren't you standing in line, slobs?' Then men would dash away in a wave. Stung by the blow, his victim would put a hand to his neck and wipe away the blood, but he'd hold his tongue, for fear of the cells" (p. 41). Prisoners are sent out to work in temperatures of twenty-seven degrees below zero and then ordered to undress to make sure that they are not wearing any clothing besides regulation dress. Buinovsky protests:

> "You've no right to strip men in the cold. You don't know Article Nine of the Criminal Code."
> But they did have the right. They knew the code. You, friend, are the one who doesn't know it.
> "You're not behaving like Soviet people," Buinovsky went on saying. "You're not behaving like communists." [p. 44]

For that protest, Volkovoi sentences the naval commander to ten days of solitary confinement.

> Brick walls, cement floor, no windows, a stove they lit only to melt the ice on the walls and make pools on the floor. You slept on bare boards, and if you'd any teeth left to eat with after all the chattering they'd be

27

doing, they gave you nine ounces of bread day after
day and hot stew only on the third, sixth, and ninth.

Ten days. Ten days "hard" in the cells—if you sat
them out to the end, your health would be ruined for
the rest of your life. T.B. and nothing but hospital for
you till you kicked the bucket.

As for those who got fifteen days "hard" and sat
them out—they went straight into a hole in the cold
earth. [p. 148]

The distinctions and conflicts between the "we" and
"they" are most clearly demonstrated in the relations between the camp authorities and guards on the one side and
the prisoners on the other. One of the guards comments on
the prisoners: "They don't know how to do a fucking thing
and don't want to learn. They're not worth the bread we
give them. We ought to feed them on shit" (p. 26). Prisoners can be sentenced to solitary confinement for not re-
moving their hats "to a guard five paces before passing him,
and replace it two paces after" (p. 30). The camp doctor
can only exempt two prisoners a day from work because of
illness, and all the rest must work, sick or not. The patients
in his infirmary who can stand on their feet are not left in
peace either; the doctor finds work for them to do, "fencing
the garden, laying paths, bringing soil to the flower-beds,
and, in wintertime, erecting snow barriers. Work, he [the
doctor] said, was a first-rate medicine for any illness"
(p. 33). Hierarchy and caste also continued to play their
roles. The doctor, for example, permits a prisoner, formerly

a university student of literature, one Vdovushkin, to be his medical orderly so that Vdovushkin can write freely in the camp what he could not write freely at the university. Tsezar, because he is an "intellectual" and gets two parcels a month, can bribe his way into a "cushy job, as assistant to the rate inspector" (p. 53), and so works in a warm, comfortable office while the rest of the squad does hard physical labor at the freezing construction site.

If the guards are cruel to the prisoners, the prisoners are even crueler to one another. "Who's the zek's main enemy?" Shukhov asks, then answers himself: "Another zek. If only they weren't at odds with one another—ah, what a difference that'd make!" (p. 119). The prisoners fight for bread, for porridge, for soup, for warmth, for an extra piece of clothing, in a war of all against all to survive. One prisoner, working with the camp authorities, even beats the other zeks when they line up hungrily to enter the mess hall—beats them with a birch club. When, at the end of the work day, the *zeks* at the construction site are held there because one prisoner is "missing" in the head count, they are furious. A Moldavian zek, working in the warmth of the repair shop, has fallen asleep and the other zeks are standing in the cold, shivering and waiting. "In the crowd everybody, including Shukhov, flew into a rage. Were they going through all this for that shit, that slimy little snake, that stinking worm? . . . The frost was gathering strength for the night—and that runty bastard was missing. . . . If the guards handed him over to the zeks, they'd tear him apart, like wolves with a lamb" (pp. 111–112). When the

29

Moldavian is discovered, the "we" of the zeks asserts itself against the "they" of the authorities. A guard is about to slam the Moldavian with his rifle butt. Now the prisoners stop cursing the Moldavian, while the Moldavian's squad leader slaps him away from the guard so that the rifle butt won't reach him, and another man from his squad, a Hungarian, kicks him in the behind. There is cruelty, true; but it is mitigated by a feeling of unity against the common enemy. The zeks are furious, not only because they are standing in the cold, but because they will be too late to get on line for their letters, their packages, the dispensary, the baths, and because they are there on "their own time" and "it's no joke to rob five hundred men of over half an hour" (p. 113).

The worst prisoners are those who act on behalf of the camp authorities, either as supervisors of the zeks or as spies. The zeks, however, have grown increasingly capable of resistance. Some of the squealers have had their throats cut while in their bunks, and "the same thing had happened to an innocent zek—someone must have gone to the wrong bunk. And one squealer had run off on his own to the head of the guardhouse and they'd put him inside for safety. Amazing. . . . Nothing like that had happened in the ordinary camps. Nor here, either, up till then." [3]

When Der, "a convict himself but a foreman, the swine, who treated his fellow prisoners worse than dogs," (p. 53)

[3] P. 73. These conditions presaged the prison-camp revolts, such as the one in Vorkuta in 1953, which took place after Stalin's death.

discovers that the 104th has stolen a roll of roofing felt to seal the windows so that it will be warm enough for them to work, he threatens Tiurin with an additional sentence in camp. Tiurin and two other members of the squad, one with a spade raised as a weapon, menace Der, and Tiurin warns him: "Your time for giving terms has passed, you bastard. If you say one word, you bloodsucker, it'll be your last day on earth. Remember that" (p. 99). Intimidated, Der backs off and accepts Tiurin's suggestion that the report state that the roofing felt was already on the windows when the 104th arrived.

The convicts have almost a Luddite hatred of the machinery which enslaves them, and they frequently sabotage the machines: "For as long as Shukhov has worked with machinery the machines had either broken down or been smashed by the zeks. He'd seen them wreck a log conveyer by shoving a beam under the chain and leaning hard on it, to give themselves a breather; they were stacking log by log with never a moment to stretch their backs" (p. 101).

In his play *The Love-Girl and the Innocent,* also set in a concentration camp, Solzhenitsyn gives another dimension to the struggle between the "we" and the "they," demonstrating dramatically how the Gulag authorities use "cooperative" prisoners against "recalcitrant" ones, criminals against politicals, privileged against deprived. Particularly bitter is Solzhenitsyn's denunciation of the use of criminals to persecute politicals—characteristic of the Stalinist regime as well as of Gulag. As one character in the play, a political prisoner, remarks: "You see we're 'enemies of the people' and they're 'friends of the people.' I reckon the authorities keep them just to suck our blood. We politicals are given to them to torment. They don't separate us in the cells or in the transports. Everyone's terrified of them" (p. 95). Stalin had, since the 1920s, called the criminals "social allies" and the politicals "social enemies." Solzhenitsyn's main character and spokesman in the play remarks that it was exactly the same with those who fought in the front lines against the Nazis and were captured, whom the regime labeled enemies, and those who were thieves and murderers and remained behind the lines, who were called "social allies." Ironically, Solzhenitsyn adds that Russian writers are also biased in favor of the professional crooks, because "they're always noble at heart, they always turn out right in the end" (p. 47).

The Gulag authorities intend "to suppress mercilessly . . . all feelings of right and legality in man [and] did not allow the convicts to forget even for a moment that they were deprived of rights, and that arbitrariness was their only judge," [4] yet the men struggle to retain some humanity. As a result, even in the Darwinian war of all against all, of men "red in tooth and claw" fighting one another, there also appears mutual aid of the Kropotkin variety. Men do work together, help each other, and not only because they are egged on by Gulag, tempted by privileges or better

[4] V. Lakshin, "Ivan Denisovich, His Friends and Foes," *Novy mir*, Jan. 1964.

rations; they sometimes work together out of a sense of craftsmanship and cooperation. More often, it is true, they work in a spirit of individual and group competition. In *Ivan Denisovich*, Solzhenitsyn writes: "Everything was so arranged in the camp that the prisoners egged one another on. . . . You're loafing, you bastard—do you think I'm willing to go hungry just because of you? Put your guts into it, slob" (p. 64). Sometimes, as when the members of the 104th turn on Der to protect Tiurin, they cooperate out of desperation.

If anything does solace the prisoners in the camp, beyond the meager comforts of food and rest and warmth that the authorities provide, it is work and religion. "Real jail," Ivan Denisovich reflects, "was when you were kept back from work" (p. 21). Once they get to work, Shukhov's instinct of workmanship takes hold, and he is able to forget the discomforts of cold and damp and hunger, "seeing only his wall. . . . His thoughts and his eyes were feeling their way under the ice to the wall itself, the outer façade of the power station, two blocks thick. At the spot he was working on, the wall had previously been laid by some mason who was either incompetent or had stunk up the job. But now Shukhov tackled the wall as if it was his own handiwork" (p. 93). He straightens the bellies in it, levels it, sets the chipped and broken bricks in properly, and as the wall rises, nothing else seems to matter. Long after the other squads have quit working, and even though his squad may be put into solitary for arriving late when the escort guards come to take them back to the camp from the work site, Shukhov goes on working, because he cannot bear to waste the mortar they have mixed.

> Wasn't it enough that Tiurin had told them himself not to bother about the mortar? Just throw it over the wall and fuck off. But Shukhov wasn't made that way —eight years in a camp couldn't change his nature. He worried about anything he could make use of, about every scrap of work he could do—nothing must be wasted without good reason. . . .
>
> But Shukhov—and if the guards had put the dogs on him it would have made no difference—ran to the back and looked about. Not bad. Then he ran and gave the wall a good look over. . . . His eye was as accurate as a carpenter's level. Straight and even. His hands were as young as ever. [pp. 105–106]

Having done a good and skillful job, Shukhov has affirmed and confirmed his worth and manliness.

"Religions" of three different varieties help some of the men to survive the rigors of camp life. Alyosha the Baptist's Christian faith gives him the strength and purpose to continue; Buinovsky's Communist idealism buoys him up; and Tsezar's commitment to art—the art of cinema— sustains him. For Alyosha the camp is a place of Christian trial, where his beliefs, his faith, can be tested. He rebukes Shukhov for praying infrequently and inadequately, saying, "That's why your prayers stay unanswered. One must never stop praying. If you have real faith you tell a mountain to move and it will move" (p. 154). Denisovich, however, has never seen a mountain at all, much less seen it move, and he doubts that all the Baptist prayers ever moved a single peak in the Caucasus. Alyosha tells him that he must not pray for material or mortal things, except for "our daily bread," and that he ought not even to pray to be freed from the camp: "Why do you want freedom? In freedom your last grain of faith will be choked with weeds. You should rejoice that you're in prison.: Here you have time to think about your soul" (p. 156). Shukhov doesn't want to contemplate his soul; for him freedom means going home, but he doesn't think the authorities will ever permit that. Instead, even if they do not give him another sentence when he has served his term, they will condemn him to exile. Painfully, he replies to Alyosha: "Jesus Christ wanted you to sit in prison and so you are—sitting there for His sake. But for whose sake am *I* here? Because we weren't ready for war in forty-one? For that? But was that *my* fault?" (p. 157). (The theme of Stalin's failure to prepare adequately for the Nazi invasion is one to which Solzhenitsyn returns again and again, almost obsessively.) Though Alyosha, eyes glowing like candles, tries to persuade Ivan Denisovich to let his soul pray, Shukhov insists: "Prayers are like those appeals of ours. Either they don't get through or they're returned with 'rejected' scrawled across 'em." Yet Shukhov himself believes in God and does pray, when the day is over, thankfully: "Glory be to Thee, O Lord. Another day over. Thank You I'm not spending tonight in the cells. Here it's still bearable" (p. 154). He likes and respects Alyosha and cannot understand what harm the Baptists could have done by praying to God that justified the regime's sentencing them to twenty-five years in concentration camps. Not only was Alyosha a man who could be relied on, who kept his mouth shut; even in the camp he was happy.

> What had he to be happy about? His cheeks were sunken, he lived strictly on his rations, he earned nothing. He spent all his Sundays muttering with the other Baptists. They shed the hardships of camp life like water off a duck's back. [p. 51]

> You could count on Alyosha. Did whatever was asked of him. If everybody in the world was like that, Shukhov would have done likewise. If a man asks for help why not help him? Those Baptists had something there. [p. 102]

In the conflict between Darwinism and Kropotkinism, between idealism and disinterestedness on the one hand and materialism and self-interest on the other, Solzhenitsyn sees an essential conflict in society and in the nature of man; and fictionally it is a source of tension the novelist continues to exploit.

Denisovich even learns that the "steel-chested" squad leader Tiurin believes in a benevolent deity. Years after he was persecuted and driven out of the army, he meets his former squadron commander, the man who had thrown him out for being the son of a kulak, and learns that his persecutor was sentenced to ten years too. "The regimental commander and the commissar," Tiurin recounts, "were both

shot in thirty-seven, no matter whether they were of pro-
letarian or kulak stock, whether they had a conscience or
not. So I crossed myself and said: 'So, after all, Creator,
You do exist up there in heaven. Your patience is long-
suffering but You strike hard' " (p. 87).

Shukhov also respects and admires Buinovsky for his
scientific knowledge and for his Communist ideals, though
he himself believes in neither. The naval commander, he
recognizes, has both character and courage, but has not yet
achieved any real understanding of what camp life requires.
Even his defense of "socialist legality" while berating the
guards for stripping the prisoners during a body search in
the Arctic weather is a kind of stupidity, almost an invitation to death. For all his admiration, Shukhov looks on
such actions askance. His eight years of experience in the
camps have taught him that it is "better to growl and submit. If you were stubborn they broke you" (p. 57). Never
does Solzhenitsyn use the "they" more meaningfully in differentiating the ruled from the rulers, the prisoners from the
guards, the people from the regime. What Shukhov recognizes is that survival is the issue, and one must decide on
the terms: foolish resistance on points of "law" is stupid;
resistance in the form of not cooperating with the authorities, of avoiding punishment, of retaining one's hold on
oneself and one's values is what is important. It is not an intellectual's view, or a Communist's: it is a Russian peasant's
and, therefore, very likely a more generally held view.

> Old Bolsheviks . . . , while praising *One Day*, point
> out that there was more to the labor-camp story than

fatalistic acceptance. The innocent Ivans, unprotesting and mild, were the majority; but there were others, more politically sophisticated, who refused to accept the injustices of the system which had sent them, guiltless, into the labor camps, and who refused to cooperate in any way with the authorities.

Unlike Ivan, they took no simple pride in getting through another day and building a fine wall. They planned and occasionally tried to carry out revolts. They called themselves the Blacks; they called the Ivans the Reds.[5]

But Solzhenitsyn was portraying "all" Russia in that simple, honest peasant-carpenter-mason, Ivan Denisovich, and he knew, from his own experience as well as from the experiences of millions who had known the camps during the Stalinist decades, that most of the Blacks perished and that some of the Reds perished—although very likely he would have refused to accept such color designations (rightly) for either group. Even such presumably sophisticated observers as Galina Serebryakova [6] and Evgenia Ginzburg [7] never

[5] Kalb, Introduction to *Ivan Denisovich*, pp. 10–11.

[6] *Sandstorm* was originally serialized in *Literaturnaya rossiya* in 1964, and then published in Paris by *Kultura* in 1967. Mrs. Serebryakova issued a public statement condemning the *Kultura* publication, insisting that it was without her permission. The *Kultura* editors indicated that they had gotten sets of page proofs which were smuggled out of the USSR from which they had published their edition.

[7] *Journey into the Whirlwind*, trans. Paul Stevenson and Max Hayward (New York: Harcourt, Brace & World, 1967).

seemed, at least in their published books, to be able to indict the Communist Party, the entire Soviet system, but took refuge in such euphemistic subterfuges as "errors," "distortions," "violations of Socialist legality," and the ubiquitous "cult of personality."

Yet, though Solzhenitsyn portrays Denisovich as a man with a survivalist ethic, it is not survival on any terms. Denisovich has notions of dignified conduct which he does not abandon; he retains his humanity, and perhaps, in Solzhenitsyn's eyes, even helps himself to survive. The novelist implies as much when he portrays the jackal Fetiukov as a man who, though he will do anything to live, is marked for death precisely because he does not have enough moral stamina.

There is a vicious irony in Solzhenitsyn's demonstration of Tsezar's commitment to the religion of art. The significant scene has a number of deliberate ironies but is technically awkward because the author chooses to present the scene as it is perceived by Ivan Denisovich; and it is difficult to believe that the peasant Shukhov would either be interested enough to listen to the whole debate or would even understand its terms. Solzhenitsyn sends Shukhov to give Tsezar his supper, to bring a bowl of cold kasha (buckwheat mush) from the kitchen to the warm office in which Tsezar is debating the merits of Sergey Eisenstein's film *Ivan the Terrible* with a nameless old prisoner, X 123. Shukhov waits for the highly intellectual debate to end so that, perhaps, Tsezar will deign to give him the kasha to eat, relinquishing the prison fare for the food he has just received in a parcel. So while Tsezar talks about Eisenstein's film as a work of genius, Shukhov, cold, tired, and hungry, waits like a dog for a bone:

> "Ham," said X 123 angrily. . . . "It's all so arty there's no art left in it. Spice and poppyseed instead of everyday bread and butter! And then, that vicious political idea—the justification of personal tyranny. A mockery of the memory of three generations of Russian intelligentsia." . . .
>
> "But what other interpretation could he [Eisenstein] have gotten away with?" [Tsezar asks].
>
> "Gotten away with? Ugh! Then don't call him a genius! Call him an ass-kisser, obeying a vicious dog's order. Geniuses don't adjust their interpretations to suit the taste of tyrants!" [p. 84]

Anyone reading those words of X 123 who has also read Solzhenitsyn's letters and his speeches to the Writers' Union knows that this is the novelist speaking in his own voice, speaking not only with a rigorous artistic criterion that refuses to rule out personal and political morality, but also with contempt for all those artists who helped to justify Stalin's tyranny and contribute to the "cult of personality."

In rendering Ivan Denisovich's day and the day of his fellow prisoners, Solzhenitsyn pictures the Stalinist decades of Soviet history, the ravages which the Stalinist-induced upheavals inflicted on the people: the collectivization of the countryside and the accompanying mass murder of kulaks in the early 1930s; the great purges of the Party and the armed forces between 1936 and 1939; the failure to prepare for World War II and the ensuing defeats, from 1941 to 1943 in the war against the Nazis; and the revived Stalinism at the end of the war and during the postwar period, with its imprisonment of former Russian prisoners of war, its repressive Zhdanov decrees, its anti-Semitic and paranoid Doctors' Plot. Over all the carnage is the specter of the political police; Russia is ruled by a madman and a tyrant whose bludgeon is the NKVD, the Cheka, the MGB, the KGB—whatever the initials of the political police are at the moment—and its adjunct, Gulag, the concentration camps' administration.

The greatest Stalinist horror is the condemning of whole *categories* of people—kulaks, prisoners captured by the Germans during the war, ethnic minorities, members of the former opposition parties—en masse to degradation, imprisonment, death. Through Alyosha, Solzhenitsyn shows how various religious believers were sentenced because they refused to give up their religions or resisted government attempts to control or destroy their faiths. Through the various minority groups in the book, particularly the Balts—Estonians, Latvians, and Lithuanians—whom Denisovich admires, Solzhenitsyn gives some inkling of the persecution and suffering these groups endured. "Well, it's said that nationality doesn't mean anything and that every nation has its bad eggs," Shukhov thinks. "But among all the Estonians . . . he'd never met a bad one" (p. 56). Solzhenitsyn is particularly bitter about the treatment of Russian combat

veterans and prisoners of war during and after World War
II. Subsuming Stalin's paranoid "logic" in dealing with
prisoners of war is the notion that contact with foreign
countries, especially Western ones, is "contaminating," de-
stroys one's "socialist purity and reliability." War prisoners were, therefore, swept up by the Soviet political
police and put into the camps for "trafficking with the
enemy," or like Ivan Denisovich, for committing "treason,"
because they had been captured by the Germans and had
either escaped or eventually been liberated by Russian or
Allied armies. Buinovsky has been jailed simply for having
received a souvenir from a British admiral with whom he
served, on Russian naval orders, as a liaison officer during
the war. Senka Klevshin, who was deafened in the campaign
of 1941, was captured by the Nazis and sent to Buchenwald. After escaping from there, he is recaptured and works
with the Communist underground in Buchenwald smug-
gling arms in for the mutiny against the Nazis. Yet he, too,
is suspect and has been sentenced to the Soviet prison
camps; his having been hung by the wrists and flogged by
the Germans for his Buchenwald resistance in no way
lessens his "culpability."

Through the squad leader Tiurin, Solzhenitsyn shows
how a gifted and essentially patriotic man, discharged
from the army, is driven in desperation to turn his brother
over to thieves to be trained to survive, and is finally har-
ried into the camps for the best part of his life because he
is the son of a kulak. Even more poignantly, Solzhenitsyn
tells the story of the persecution of the kulaks through

Lyuba, the "love-girl" of the play *The Love-Girl and the Innocent*, who recalls what happened to her and to her kulak family:

LYUBA: I was six. I remember a huge barge full of dispossessed *kulak* farmers. There were no partitions in the hold, no tiered bunks. People just lay on top of other people. Maybe it was because I was small, but the walls of the barge seemed to tower over me like cliffs. Guards with guns walked round the top edge. Our whole family was exiled, but our two elder brothers weren't living with us, so they weren't touched. They came to the transit camp . . . on the look-out for a chance to get their family out of trouble. They didn't succeed. But they managed to buy me from the escort commander. They gave him a shirt with a zip—they were just coming into fashion. I don't remember how they got me off the barge, but I remember we were in a little boat, and the water shone brightly in the sun.

NEMOV: What about your parents?

LYUBA: They died up beyond the Arctic Circle. They starved to death. They were dumped in the naked tundra. How could they survive?

. . . . .

You can't imagine how we lived after that. I had no room, so I lived five years in a bit of dark corridor. There was no window and I couldn't do my homework after school. I went to school every day hungry and dressed like a beggar. I couldn't complain or ask for help in case people found out we were *kulaks.* . . . They married me off when I was fourteen. [pp. 104–105]

(In the nonfictional account of his own imprisonment, *My Testimony*, Anatoly Marchenko recounts the story of a kulak, Anatoly Burov, whom he met in the concentration camps. The story is almost identical with the fictional account Solzhenitsyn puts in Lyuba's mouth. The similarity, I suspect, is due neither to indebtedness nor coincidence, but simply to the mass character of the Stalinist campaign against the kulaks and the consistently vicious methods employed against them. Burov's story could be multiplied by the millions:

He had still been quite small, about two or three years old, when his family were proclaimed "kulaks" and dispossessed. All he remembered was how he and the other children, together with his mother and father and blind grandmother, had been driven out into the winter snow in what they stood up in. Somehow they got by till spring in somebody or other's cowshed, and then in spring all the dispossessed families were rounded up, loaded on to a steamer and transported down the river Ob. They were put ashore on the deserted bank, hundreds of miles from the nearest habitation, and left to fend for themselves as best they could. . . .

At first they dug pits for themselves, then they began to fell trees, build homes and clear the land of undergrowth. With tremendous difficulty they adapted themselves to this new spot and got some sort of small farms going. Sometimes about five or six of the men would get together and go off secretly "to the mainland," take jobs to earn extra money and bring back cattle, tools, utensils. About three to four years later the steamer returned with officials on board [who] walked from house to house and inspected the farms and ploughed fields. They were amazed! There were supposed to be only graves. Just look at those damned kulaks! Exploiters, and even here they manage to survive! The powers that be . . . in two months returned together with . . . a multitude of armed soldiers . . . and proceeded once more to dispossess the kulaks: everyone was thrown out of his home, being allowed to take not even a pot or pan along with him, herded on to the steamer and transported further.) [8]

Solzhenitsyn believes that some measure of freedom can, finally, be achieved in the concentration camps, that the imprisonment of the body cannot ultimately imprison the spirit. Denisovich reflects:

One good thing about these "special" camps—you were free to let off steam. At Ust-Izhma you need

[8] Anatoly Marchenko, *My Testimony* (New York: Dutton, 1969), pp. 50–51.

45

only whisper that there was a shortage of matches outside, and they'd put you in the guardhouse and add another ten years to your stretch. But here you could bawl anything you liked from the top row of bunks—the squealers didn't pass it on, the security boys had stopped caring. [p. 141]

Therefore, prisoner X 123 can call Eisenstein an ass-kisser openly and Stalin a tyrant, and another nameless prisoner can say of Stalin's pitiless paranoia: "D'you mean to say you think Old Whiskers [Stalin] will take pity on you? Why, he wouldn't trust his own brother. You haven't a chance, you ass" (p. 141). And Alyosha and his fellow Baptists can, at last, find a place in which they can pray. Perhaps (although this is not clear) Solzhenitsyn is saying that even in the worst society—a concentration camp— some degree of freedom can be salvaged from tyranny if one is prepared to sacrifice almost everything else for it: home, family, work, education, most of what constitutes "normal" life. Or is he declaring, like that old Christian adage, that if one would find oneself, one must first lose oneself?

Over all of Russian society and Russian history there looms the specter of the penal colony, of the informer, the torturer and interrogator, the camp guard. Solzhenitsyn is speaking of the whole Soviet Union as a concentration camp when he has one of his characters in *The Love-Girl* say: "Forget the outside world. Life has different laws in here. This is Campland, an invisible country.

It's not in the geography books, or the psychology books or the history books. This is the famous country where ninety-nine men weep while one man laughs" (p. 34). No one is or was immune to persecution by the political police on arbitrary and concocted grounds—and there is neither law nor leniency to help the persecuted. And normal human relations are poisoned by the constant fear and terror, the use of informers and blackmail. Shurochka, in *The Love-Girl*, one of the decent women convicted and sent to the camps for refusing to become an informer— one can be convicted for *having failed to report* an "objectionable" conversation to the KGB—asks the "Innocent," Nemov: "Tell me, what is it that makes people in the camps so horrible? Were they different outside? Or were they just lying low?" (p. 49). But Solzhenitsyn answers the question implicitly rather than explicitly by demonstrating that the way people behave in the camps is not very different from the way they behave outside, nor are the rules of life on the outside very different from those inside the camp: terror, coercion, informing, corruption are everywhere. Yet the people in the camps are, nevertheless, much worse off. The long sentences, often ten to twenty-five years, the two letters a year prisoners can send and receive, the infrequent parcels, the difficulties of arranging for visits, the regime's pressures on the families of zeks deliberately aimed at the cutting men off from their homes and families, and from the "outside" world. Conditions in the camps make the world outside seem unreal and abnormal. The camp becomes the omni-

47

present and omnivorous reality, because most of the zeks have little hope of surviving their sentences and do not believe that they will be released even if they do serve out their time; they think that some pretext will be found to extend their original sentences. Their sentences seem to be for life, and these life sentences give to Solzhenitsyn's use of the camp as a metaphor for all Soviet life even greater force and intensity.

By a quirk of history, *Ivan Denisovich* appeared on the hundredth anniversary of the publication of Dostoyevsky's *House of the Dead*. Both a defender of the regime, Aleksandr Dymshits, and a Yugoslav regime critic, Mihajlo Mihajlov, compare Solzhenitsyn's novel to Dostoyevsky's. In *Literatura i zhizn* (November 28, 1962), Dymshits tries to place the entire blame for the camps on Stalin and to portray them as a "transient phenomenon," a passing distortion of "socialist legality." Yet he carefully skirts the fact that this "transient phenomenon" has been an intrinsic part of most of Soviet history to date, that even by the most lenient standards it has touched and permanently scarred millions of victims and their families. Mihajlov's essay, originally published in Serbo-Croat in the Zagreb journal *Forum* (No. 6, 1964), and reprinted in his book *Russian Themes*, compares prison conditions in Russia during the nineteenth and twentieth centuries, as exemplified in *Ivan Denisovich* and *House of the Dead*, and demonstrates that the Czar's prisons were far more humane than Stalin's and, of course, had only a fraction of the number of political prisoners.

Boris Dyakov's *Endured*, published in Vsevolod Kochetov's *Oktyabr* in July 1964, was a nonfictional account of
the Stalinist camps by a former inmate, which, like Galina
Serebryakova's *Sandstorm* and Evgenia Ginzburg's *Journey into the Whirlwind*, attempted to show that prisoners
retained their faith in Communist ideals, in the Party and
its leadership, and ultimately in Soviet justice. "The
strength of B. Dyakov's story," the conservative editors
of *Oktyabr* proclaimed, "lies in the fact that it is about
real Soviet people, true Communists. Even under arduous
conditions, they did not lose their human dignity: they
were true to their Party ideals and devoted to their country." Moreover, to give more weight to Dyakov's account
as contrasted with Solzhenitsyn's *Ivan Denisovich*, *Oktyabr's* editors carefully pointed out that there is nothing
fictitious in Dyakov's book; he "tells of what he saw with
his own eyes, what he himself experienced. His heroes are
real people, some dead, some still alive." [9]

Dyakov nonetheless, gives a scarifying picture of the
camps. He shows men who beg for death, doctors who
commit suicide by slashing their throats with glass shards,
men who are told that they are nothing—and then reduced
to nothing. One of the guards, a Sergeant Nelga, informs
the prisoners that they are no longer people: "No! You
are criminals. . . . Question: why are you criminals?
Answer: Because you have committed a crime." The camp
security officer, Kalashnikov, asks Dyakov what he believes

[9] "The Isolation of Soviet Literature," *Bulletin of the Institute
for the Study of the USSR*, Oct. 1964, p. 34 (hereafter referred
to as *Bulletin*).

his rights are, and Dyakov replies: "I have no rights at all, except the right to think." To which the KGB man replies, "Go away. We will even sentence you for your thoughts!" [10]

Despite this Orwellian dialogue, Dyakov's work is dedicated to justifying the Party and to explaining away the Stalinist terror. Though he never succeeds in doing more than making a leap into faith—faith in the Party, in Soviet legality—Dyakov has one of the leading personalities in his memoir, a man who has spent eighteen years in the camps, remark:

> You and I have been cruelly treated. A terrible and fantastic error has been made. But after all, it is the people who are erring; the Party will succeed in overcoming their errors, no matter how highly placed those guilty of these criminal errors may be. I believe this, I believe it! This is what gives me patience. . . . Comrade, Leninist truth lives on in our Party.[11]

Aside from this *O altitudo!* of faith and the casuistry of a logic which blames the people rather than the Party for what was inflicted on them, Dyakov's intention to free the Party and the institutions of Soviet life of responsibility for the crimes rings hollow. Even by Marxist standards the logic leaves much to be desired: how, for example, could such "distortions" as Stalinism and the camps arise in a "socialist system"? And if they did, what happened to the "leading role" of the Party and its omniscient

[10] *Ibid.*, p. 35.   [11] *Ibid.*, p. 36.

infallibility? Why, in the two decades of Stalin's absolute control, did the Party do nothing, and only three years after the dictator's death at last openly criticize his madness and murder? How the Party permitted such crimes and still remains infallible is not explained, nor is the question even addressed—nor why Party leaders who, at least formally, were Stalin's equals took no action against him and his crimes until after his death. If, moreover, the "superstructure" arises from the "base," then how could such crimes arise from "socialist production relations"?

Marchenko's *My Testimony*, written in 1967, is more honest and impressive than Dyakov's acount. Marchenko was a prisoner in the same camp in which Solzhenitsyn was confined and in which he set *Ivan Denisovich*. Marchenko completed a six-year sentence in 1966, so his account demonstrates that the camps have continued substantially unchanged during the fifteen years since Stalin's demise. Like Dyakov, Marchenko avers that he invented neither a single person or incident, and his unvarnished, documentary account not only lends credibility to his testimony, but also shows the superiority of Solzhenitsyn's art. Fiction can be truer than fact.

Almost everyone during Marchenko's time in camp had been sentenced in a closed court, and the majority had not even been shown a record of their sentences; it had only been read to them.[12] Zeks were still taken to work by armed escort guards and dogs; the work was hard and bitter, the food poor, and there were marked-off zones

[12] *My Testimony*, p. 42.

where guards would shoot prisoners without warning. Marchenko tells how convicts grew so desperate that they slit their veins, swallowed barbed wire, sprinkled ground glass in their eyes. Men were still sentenced to the "cooler" for a solitary confinement that frequently left them wrecks. Men deliberately feigned escape attempts so that they would be shot dead by the guards. Prisoners tattooed themselves with anti-Communist slogans, out of hatred for the regime which imprisoned and tormented them: "Communists equal butchers"; "Slave of the CPSU"; "Lenin was a butcher." On one man's throat was tattooed a hand, on the back of which was written "CPSU." Another man tattooed his ear with "A gift to the 22d Congress of the CPSU," then cut the ear off and threw it to one of his jailers. The camps' horror stories give some indication of the desperation of the inmates and tend to confirm the idea that those who "find freedom" there are a very small group. [13]

Marchenko recounts an interesting story about Solzhenitsyn's work. At a political indoctrination session for zeks, the top KGB officer at the camp, a Major Postnikov, denounced Solzhenitsyn. "Your Solzhenitsyn distorts life! My two daughters—at school both of them—went and read *Ivan Denisovich* and then imagined that they could start criticizing their father. Questions, reproaches, tears almost every evening! In the beginning I explained it all to them nicely, but later I had to throw the magazine [*Novy mir*] on the fire and that was the end of it." [14] No simpler,

[13] See *My Testimony*, pp. 90–94, 140–143, *passim*.
[14] *Ibid.*, p. 319.

more stark account of the problem of the heirs of Stalin and of fathers and sons—albeit in this case father and daughters—can be imagined. For what Major Postnikov symbolizes is the fear of the political police that, as heirs of Stalin, questions, reproaches, and criticisms will ultimately lead to revelations, trials, and punishments for their crimes. The KGB major, therefore, wishes to throw such novels as *Ivan Denisovich* on the fire so that the next generation—the sons—will have no evidence with which to contradict their fathers' professions of innocence.

Solzhenitsyn not only staked out new territory for contemporary Soviet writers by dealing directly and candidly with the camps in *One Day in the Life of Ivan Denisovich;* he also explored new terrain in the use of language, exploiting a combination of prison, peasant, and pornographic slang unusual in the idiom of Soviet books. Especially objectionable to such conservatives as Kochetov, for example, was his use of the four-letter words and the "mother-oath" words for which Russian is notorious. Yet his use of colloquial speech is both apt and powerful, and he never uses vulgar language for show or pointlessly.

> Ivan Denisovich is a peasant and mixes mostly with peasants, but in the camp there are also officers, soldiers and criminals. Moreover, the world they live in is cut off from the world outside. It is not surprising, therefore, if the language they speak has grown wild, so to speak, and primitive; what is noteworthy is that is has managed to preserve its traditional expres-

siveness, its power of inventing new words and images, and its popular humor—now become macabre.

The use of such language is an element in Solzhenitsyn's desire for greater naturalness and sincerity in telling his story and in characterizing his people; "Solzhenitsyn had to deal with the language of a kolkhoznik which had become mixed with the vocabulary of citydwellers and pungent expressions derived from thieves' cant." [15] The style, the subject matter, and the characterization are perfectly suited to one another, and only when Solzhenitsyn wishes to incorporate into the story more complex and abstract material—such as Tsezar's discussion of Eisenstein's cinematography with Prisoner X 123—does the combination of the three reveal some shortcomings.

The sober, documentary tone, the swift brush-stroke characterization, shrewd but not—with the exception of Ivan Denisovich—profound, the fleeting descriptions and functional dialogue are all elements of an endeavor to maintain a quiet voice. There is a deliberate refusal of sensationalism, of the desire to shock; Solzhenitsyn never stoops to melodrama; he never exaggerates; he never pushes the horrors of the camps to their bitter end. In fact, he deliberately chooses a relatively good day in Ivan Denisovich's life in the camp, "a day without a dark cloud. Almost a happy day" (p. 159). Precisely in that refusal to go beyond the daily mundane facts is the novel's great power;

[15] V. Zavalishin, "Solzhenitsyn, Dostoevsky, and Leshenkov-Klychkov," *Bulletin*, Nov. 1963, p. 41.

by carefully sticking to those facts, by his macabre humor, by his irony and understated sense of horror, Solzhenitsyn gives an even greater reality to the cruelty of the camps, to the systematic criminality of the Soviet penal system, than a shriller voice would, than emphasis on the killing, the suicides, the self-mutilation, the torture would.

> Solzhenitsyn's art does not lie in any external embellishments tacked on to the idea and the content for effect. No, it lies precisely in the flesh and blood of the work, its soul. It may seem to the unsophisticated reader that he has before him a piece of life torn straight from its depths and left just as it is—alive, quivering, with tattered edges, dripping.[16]

But just as there is power in so defining and confining his indignation, so too there is limitation. In restricting himself to a documentary tone, to a first-person account given by a kolkhoz peasant who has great guile but little knowledge and sophistication, Solzhenitsyn deliberately narrows the scope of the novel. In confining himself within the bounds of Ivan Denisovich's sensibility, the novelist willingly sacrifices a more profound point of view in order to create symbolically an innocent Ivan. Shukhov is perhaps the Russian peasant at his best: the epitome of the simple and decent countryman, hard-working and skillful with his hands, shrewd and sensible, ignorant but cunning when necessary; neither vicious nor violent, he is responsible and compassionate; he automatically detests the Soviet method

16 Lakshin, "Ivan Denisovich, His Friends and Foes."

of "one man works, one man watches" (p. 97), and would, as he remarks of Alyosha and the Baptists, help another man if that man asked him for help. If there is in Solzhenitsyn's portrait of Shukhov some of the old Populist hope for the peasant as the regenerating factor in Russian life, there is none of that *Narodnaya volya* (People's Will) sentimentality about the peasant; he knows peasants too well, and Denisovich is therefore neither a paragon nor what the Soviet orthodox critics like to call a "positive hero." There is in Shukhov peasant deference, peasant superstition, peasant ignorance, peasant passive resistance. For him, as perhaps for most of Russia's citizens, the problem is how to get through a single day, each day, one day —hence the aptness of the title. To Ivan Denisovich, life neither in the camp nor outside it makes much sense; the failures of the Soviet leadership to prepare for World War II, his own unjust imprisonment as well as that of millions of others, and the crass success of the money-making carpet painters of his home kolkhoz are all incomprehensible. What is necessary for Ivan Denisovich and all the innocent Ivans is simply to endure it all and survive. For more intelligent and complex personalities, such as Tsezar or Buinovsky or Prisoner X 123, it is not enough merely to survive the day, or even to seize it; they must make sense of their experiences, understand the relationships between ends and means, cause and effect; they must integrate the one day with the many, with the years and the "current of history," must see some pattern or meaning in what is happening to them, to their country, and to the world. In all these things they must seek an answer to the most important of the "accursed questions" that have plagued Russian writers: How is one to live? How is life to be organized? What are good and evil?

In confining himself to Ivan Denisovich's consciousness, in carefully hewing to fact in dealing with the holocaust of Stalinist terror, purge, and concentration camp, Solzhenitsyn opposes the tendency to falsify, inflate, and distort reality either by "lacquering" or by using the overblown rhetoric so endemic in officially approved Soviet writing. In speaking of the unspeakable, Solzhenitsyn is saying, one must show an ascetic restraint in choosing one's words. Yet the strengths are also weaknesses, for they prevent the book from transcending the boundaries of the specifically Soviet experience to a general experience; in brief, the camp is a metaphor for Russian life but not for most of human life elsewhere. Some critics have nonetheless tried to see the book as more than it is in this respect.

> It is as symbolic of human existence as is Kafka's *Trial.* The one day in the life of Ivan Denisovich is a day in *anybody's* life. The majority of the human race are trapped in a monstrous daily routine which differs from that of a concentration camp only in the *degree* of its unpleasantness and hopelessness. Solzhenitsyn exhibits a peculiarly Russian genius for transmuting the monotonous and sordid into a parable about human existence in general.[17]

[17] Max Hayward, "Epilogue," in *Soviet Literature in the Sixties,* ed. Max Hayward and Edward L. Crowley (London:

Such overstatement asks more of the book than it is able to provide, and in some measure therefore denigrates what it can and does provide. However unpleasant and tragic the lives of the largest part of mankind may be, they are not trapped in the gruesome ways in which Gulag traps its zeks; and it is precisely in terms of the *degree* of difficulty that men encounter in life that their lives and societies must be measured.

In creating Ivan Denisovich Shukhov, Solzhenitsyn seems to be aiming at "a kind of radical moral therapy, by treating national traumas in terms that cut through all the usual abstractions, sophistries and silences in order to reassert the primacy of intimate, individual human experience." [18] In that portrait, Solzhenitsyn may seem to show a lack of sophistication and of a sense of complexity and ambiguity, but perhaps he sees beyond those to an organic wholeness and goodness that "sophistication," especially the Western variety, finds embarrassing in their apparent simplicity. The banality of evil has been accepted widely; so, too, perhaps the banality of good is agreed upon, but goodness is

---

Methuen, 1965), p. 206. This is one of the rare instances in which Hayward's level-headedness deserts him and leads him into critical hyperbole: *Ivan Denisovich* cannot, I believe, lay claim to the kind of universality of *The Trial* or *The Castle;* nor do I think there is a peculiarly *Russian* genius for transmuting the monotonous and sordid into literary parable. Many significant literatures contain writers who do that with their own "peculiar" national and individual genius.

[18] Donald Fanger, "Solzhenitsyn: Ring of Truth," *The Nation,* Oct. 7, 1968.

not at all banal but altogether extraordinary, however banal it may appear. If the novel succeeds, as in great measure it does, it is perhaps because it renders that insight; and if it fails, as in some measure it also does, it may be because the experiences Solzhenitsyn chose to deal with cannot be contained in the vessel he used. It may be that literary realism in characterization and language is insufficient to encompass the monstrosities, absurdities, and grotesqueries that Stalinism and Hitlerism have brought to modern life.

3 ⚡ Squaring the Circle:
⚡ The Potemkin Facade

> Have you ever noticed what makes Russian literary heroes different from the heroes of Western novels? The heroes of Western literature are always after careers, money, fame. The Russians can get along without food and drink—it's justice and good they're after.
>
> *Aleksandr Solzhenitsyn*

As *One Day* portrays a single day in January 1951 in a bleak Siberian concentration camp—one day during the sentence of a peasant intended to symbolize all of Russia's innocent Ivans—so *The First Circle* portrays four days in December 1949 in the lives of a quite different class of prisoners—Soviet intelligentsia—and quite different circumstances of imprisonment. Yet the two books are inextricably tied together, for only with the menace of the concentration camp in the background do the decisions and lives of the characters in *The First Circle* take on meaning and perspective. The novel's setting is the Mavrino Special Prison, a technical and research institute on the outskirts of Moscow which, in Soviet slang, is called a *sharashka* (a corrupt institution which has a sham respectable front) and is staffed by prisoners who are physicists, mathematicians, engineers, and technicians, all working on a special electronics project under the baleful supervision of the political police. The *sharashka* is the "first circle of hell." The prisoners are precariously poised on the lip of the abyss; a single misstep can send them plunging to the lowest depths of hell—the concentration camps of Norilsk, Perm, Chita, Pechora, Vorkuta, Karaganda, or Magadan.

The implications of the book's title suggest that Solzhenitsyn intended the "first circle" to be more than simply that level of Dante's hell to which the souls of pre-Christian philosophers were eternally doomed: rather, he intended it to be a paradigm of one level of Soviet life, which consists of different circles of hell, prisons in which all Soviet citizens serve indefinite sentences. While the term "first circle" refers to the *sharashka* as the top rung of the prison ladder, it also applies to those who rule Russia (its "ruling circle"). Solzhenitsyn is impelled to depict, as members of that circle, such actual personages as Josef Stalin; his Minister of State Security, Viktor Abakumov; his personal secretary, Lieutenant General Aleksandr Poskrebyshev; and a number of other "real" people as well as some only slightly disguised. The first circle also signifies the Soviet "new class" of Party and government elite, and its circles of courtiers and hangers-on. Furthermore, "first circle" is a metaphor for the basic family circle, which Solzhenitsyn portrays as of profound value, but in which men are also imprisoned by their love and responsibilities.

And the first circle is also the circle of man's mind, thoughts, prejudices, affections, within which man is also confined.

For those in the ruling first circle Solzhenitsyn reserves a corrosive contempt and an overwhelming disgust, and for Stalin he entertains a particularly fastidious and intense loathing. To the other circles of Soviet society, even as he judges them corrupt or evil or inadequate, he brings compassion and understanding, and makes allowances for human fear and frailty, everywhere revealing the painful search human beings essay for decency and dignity, for meaning and purpose, even in a police state.

In *One Day*, Solzhenitsyn concentrates on *physical* discomfort, the cold, hunger, and brutality imposed on the zeks in the camp; in *The First Circle*, however, he concentrates on the *psychological* and *intellectual* discomforts which the prisoners must endure. Men in the *sharashka* are neither cold nor hungry, but they are psychologically demeaned and emotionally starved, and their true intellectual bent is warped to the purposes of the regime. Consequently, the problems of survival at Mavrino are different from those in Ivan Denisovich's camp: one must be concerned not only with physical survival, but with remaining intellectually and emotionally intact. The physical heroism of ordinary men trying to stay alive in the camps is matched here by the moral and intellectual heroism of the intelligentsia trying to retain their integrity in the face of the police's pressure. Almost all of the "thinking" characters in *The First Circle* are compelled to try to make sense of their lives and to make sense of what has happened in the Soviet Union in their lifetimes, even if, in so doing, they run the risk of disillusion, disgust, cynicism, and even death—and all who do so run the risk of being put on a "transport" to one of the concentration camps in Siberia or the frozen Arctic. It is a task beyond all their capacities in a way that surviving one day was not beyond Ivan Denisovich's, but they try nonetheless.

Not only must they try to put some order into their individual and collective pasts, but during those four days in 1949, from December 24 through December 27, with Christmas and the approaching new year (Western) reminding them even more forcefully of their former lives "outside," they must also make sense of the present. Stalin is preparing to launch another great purge in the Soviet Union which, in due course, is to become the infamous Doctors' Plot of 1953. He has already precipitated the East European Communist Parties into a bloody maelstrom of arrests, trials, and executions: Wladyslaw Gomulka has been arrested in Poland; Laszlo Rajk has been tortured and murdered in Hungary; and Traicho Kostov is in the midst of a show trial in Bulgaria. Mavrino's research on secret telephonic communications is meant to play an important role in Stalin's plans and purges, and consequently each of the novel's major figures is required in those four wintry days to make some personal decision about whether or not he will accept the regime's plans and methods, and whether or not he will cooperate with its representatives, in this case the secret-police authorities who run the *sharashka*. A year earlier, the head of Mavrino, Anton Yakonov, Colonel of Engineers in the MVD (the security police), was given the task of creating a secret telephone for Stalin so that no one could understand his conversations even if they were monitored. A second device has also been assigned to Mavrino, a device which will identify the voice of anyone speaking over a telephone —a kind of aural fingerprinting mechanism to be used by the police for surveillance.

It has become urgent that the second device be completed. A Soviet diplomat, Innokenty Volodin, has telephoned the home of his childhood family physician, Dr. Dobroumov. Unable to reach the doctor because the stupid woman who answers the telephone refuses to let him through until he identifies himself, in desperation Volodin finally warns her: "When the professor was in Paris on his recent trip, he promised his French colleagues he would give them something! Some kind of medicine. And he's supposed to give it to them in a few days. To foreigners! Do you understand? He must not do it! He must not give the foreigners anything! It could be used as a provoca——." [1] The telephone call is then cut off, so Volodin is aware that the secret police have been monitoring the line. What he does not know, but suspects, is that they have also taped the conversation and now want the Mavrino technicians to help them identify the caller. Volodin had taken the precaution of calling from a public

[1] *The First Circle*, trans. Thomas P. Whitney (New York: Harper & Row, 1968), p. 5.

telephone booth, trying to disguise his voice, and though the police do not know who actually made the call, they have logically reduced the suspects to a list of the few people at the Foreign Ministry who knew about the plan to implicate Dr. Dobroumov in the plot.

The novel opens with Volodin trying to decide whether or not to make the call and then deciding to do so. The scene is full of foreboding and dramatic foreshadowing, because it is clear that the sensitive, intelligent, and decent Volodin, his French-style shoes plunging into the dirty wet Moscow snow as he searches for an out-of-the-way public telephone booth from which to call Dobroumov and passes the Great Lubyanka Prison, is going to end up in that prison before the novel ends.

> Innokenty looked up and trembled. He sensed a new meaning in the new building of the Bolshaya Lubyanka which faced on Furkasovsky Lane, and he shuddered. This nine-storied gray-black hulk was a battleship, and the eighteen pilasters hung on its starboard side like eighteen gun turrets. Solitary and frail, Innokenty was drawn toward it, across the little square, under the prow of the heavy, swift ship.

However fearful Volodin is, however much he knows the danger he is courting, he realizes that he has no other choice but to make the call: "If one is forever cautious, can one remain a human being?" (p. 3).

The second scene of the novel, immediately following, depicts a new transport of zeks being brought to Mavrino from the concentration camps. Not only is this an example of Solzhenitsyn's skillful use of ironic contrast—the diplomat beginning his descent from his first circle in the Foreign Ministry into the nether world that is the hell of Lubyanka and the camps, and the zeks coming out of the nether world of the camps up into the first circle of the Mavrino *sharashka*—it is also his introduction of the two main threads of the narrative, which together will set the warp and woof of the novel, the intertwining of the two first circles, the deliberate contrast of the "inside prison" at its best and the "outside prison" at its best—but prisons both, both circles of hell.

One Day in the Life of Ivan Denisovich was based on Solzhenitsyn's experiences in the Kazakhstan concentration camp to which he had been sentenced; in the furor created by the publication of the book, some of its characters had been "identified" with real people in that camp. *The First Circle* is rooted in Solzhenitsyn's own experience at Mavrino, to which he was sent not too long after his arrest and imprisonment.[2] The protagonist of that novel is Gleb Nerzhin, a complicated, reflective, and courageous man who bears a remarkable resemblance to his creator. Like

[2] Pavel Licko, "One Day with Solzhenitsyn—An Interview," *Soviet Survey*, July 1967, p. 184. Solzhenitsyn said: "In a questionnaire we had to fill in, I wrote that I was a mathematician and physicist. I was then taken to a prison research institute where the standard was so high that any scientist would have been proud to work there. As a prisoner mathematician I spent four of the eight years in good conditions."

Solzhenitsyn, Nerzhin is a trained mathematician, thirty-one years old (Solzhenitsyn was thirty-one in 1949, the time of the novel), who was, like Solzhenitsyn, a combat artillery officer during World War II and is a University of Rostov graduate; he is married to Nadya, a chemistry student he met at the university (Solzhenitsyn's wife Natalya was studying chemistry at Rostov when they met and married). Nerzhin was set to work on a construction site where an apartment house was being built for the political police (Solzhenitsyn worked for a year on such building sites in and around Moscow) before he was sent to Mavrino.[3] As Nerzhin is finally sent away from the *sharashka* to a camp in Siberia (where Solzhenitsyn served the last three years of his sentence, in a mining region of Kazakhstan) because he refuses to cooperate with the authorities, so too Solzhenitsyn—"I . . . could not make moral compromises"—was eventually expelled from Ma-

[3] *Ibid.*, p. 183. Solzhenitsyn told his interviewer: "I was employed on building sites near Moscow and in Moscow itself. On the Leninskii Prospekt there is a large building with turrets and a shop called Spartak on the ground floor. I worked there." In the novel, p. 21, Nerzhin remarks: "At the Kaluga Gates, in the MVD apartment house, the rounded one with the tower. Our camp was building it in 1945, and I was working as an apprentice, laying parquet floors. . . . I've been worrying ever since about my workmanship, or, if you prefer, my prestige. Do my floors squeak or don't they?" *Time*, Sept. 27, 1968, p. 23, reported: "Twenty years later, when some of the apartments [of a Moscow apartment building for secret-police officials] had been turned over to high-ranking scientists, Solzhenitsyn was invited to visit a friend in the same building. He was proud to discover that his floors did not squeak."

vrino.[4] A number of things can also be deduced about
Solzhenitsyn from what Nerzhin tells us about himself
in the novel, particularly from some passages which, both
by the nature of the material and the peculiarly intense and
authentic tone which informs it, stand out in the text. For
example, Solzhenitsyn tells how even as a boy Nerzhin
could not believe in Stalin, how he was afflicted from the
very first with his own "Emperor's New Clothes" psychology concerning the dictator.

> At the age of twelve he had gone through an
> enormous pile of *Izvestiya* as tall as he was and he
> had read about the trial of the saboteur engineers.
> From the very first, the boy did not believe what he
> read. He did not know why—his reason could not
> grasp it—but he could clearly see that it was all a lie.
> Either because his ear was young or because he
> read more than there was in the newspapers, he clearly
> sensed the falsity in the exaggerated, stifling exalta-
> tion of one man, always one man! If he was every-
> thing, did it not mean that other men were nothing?
> Out of pure protest Gleb refused to let himself be
> carried away.
> Gleb was only a ninth-grader on the December

[4] Licko, p. 184. The similarity or identity of details, great
and small, between Solzhenitsyn's autobiography as it is known
and that past which he gives to his creation Gleb Nerzhin is
noteworthy. Nonetheless, it is an error to simplify any author's
viewpoint by assigning it to any single one of his creations.
Solzhenitsyn, like any gifted artist, speaks through all his creations,
although some are "closer to him" than others.

morning when he looked into a display window where a newspaper was posted and read that Kirov had been killed. And suddenly, like a blinding light, it became clear to him that Stalin and no one else had killed Kirov. Because he was the only one who would profit by his death! A feeling of aching loneliness seized him—the grown men, crowded near him, did not understand that simple truth.

Then the same Old Bolsheviks, who had made the entire Revolution and whose whole life it had been, began by the dozens and the hundreds to drift into nonexistence. Some, not waiting to be arrested, swallowed poison in their apartments; others hanged themselves at their houses outside the city. But most let themselves be arrested and appeared in court and unaccountably confessed, loudly condemned themselves with the worst vilifications, and admitted serving in all the foreign intelligence agencies in the world. It was so overdone, so crude, so excessive, that only a stone ear could fail to hear the lie. [pp. 202–203]

The passionate loathing of Stalin is everywhere apparent in Solzhenitsyn, and especially in *The First Circle*. Solzhenitsyn almost never refers to Stalin except as the Boss, the Plowman, the Little Father, the Butcher, the Great Generalissimo, the Coryphaeus of the Sciences, the Most Brilliant Strategist of All Times and Peoples. The depth of his hatred leads Solzhenitsyn into one of his least successful characterizations, that of the dictator himself. Solzhenitsyn, in *The First Circle*, portrays Stalin as a megalomaniac full of paranoid suspicion, coarse cunning, and a brutality of sadistic proportions, a man now half-senile and altogether alone and cut off from life and people, respecting no one, trusting no one, loving no one— not even his once beloved daughter Svetlana—fearing everyone, including his most servile courtiers. Solzhenitsyn, in one shrewd and not altogether effective use of the Potemkin façade, shows Stalin having been taken in by the official image of him created by his propagandists: "The simple ordinary people love their Leader, understand him and love him. . . . That much he [Stalin] could see from the newspapers, and from the movies, and from the display of gifts. His birthday had become a national holiday, and that was good to know. How many messages there had been!" (p. 88). Crude, dull, limited, Stalin is a provincial Georgian anxious to be accepted as a Great Russian. As a result he becomes the Party expert on the nationality question: "The exile of whole nationalities was both his major theoretical contribution and his boldest experiment." [5] An anti-Semite, he delights in launching the anti-Semitic Doctors' Plot and is happy to believe that he has won Russia's heart instead of all "those famous, protesting, goateed Talmudists, kinless, rootless,

---

[5] P. 94. Why dictators often come from minority populations is a fascinating problem. Napoleon was a Corsican, Alexander the Great a Macedonian, Stalin a Georgian, to take some of the more notorious examples—and Hitler was an Austrian.

with nothing positive about them." [6] He is vengeful and sadistic; his joy is to kill. "This had always been his distinctive trait as a statesman and military leader: neither dismissal, nor ostracism, nor the insane asylum, nor life imprisonment, nor exile seemed to him sufficient punishment for a person he recognized as dangerous. *Death* was the only reliable means of settling accounts in full." [7]

Yet this man whose name fills the newspapers, after whom cities, universities, factories, and palaces have been named, is only "a little old man with a desiccated double chin which was never shown in his portraits, a mouth permeated with the smell of Turkish leaf tobacco, and fat fingers which left their traces on books" (p. 86). As King Midas turned everything to gold, so Stalin turns everyone into a mediocrity. The first circle ruling Russia is filled with mediocrities or worse: Abakumov, a strong-arm bully boy with four years of primary school education, is a skilled jujitsu expert who smashes people's faces during secret-police interrogations—which qualifies him to become Minister of State Security; Poskrebyshev is a veterinarian by profession, an orderly in talents—"His surname, which meant bread baked from scraps of dough, was justified: it was as though they had not scraped up enough qualities of mind and character when they baked

---

[6] P. 115. The reference, of course, is to the many Jews among the early Bolsheviks, particularly Trotsky, Zinovief, and Kamenev.

[7] P. 111. In this, if in nothing else, Stalin's heirs have been more lenient than Stalin, utilizing all the techniques Solzhenitsyn mentions here but not—yet—death.

him" [8]—which qualifies him to head Stalin's personal secretariat and gives him immense powers; Ryumin is a provincial accountant whose fame is based on his framing a journalist and on his cunning as a Smersh interrogator —which qualifies him to become Deputy Minister of State Security. The "historical" characters are men of small stature and vicious natures, and the fictional creations in this ruling circle are the same. Stalin chooses such men because of the limitations of his own intellect and character, because he is crass and therefore finds "self-seeking people are easier to understand and manage. Most of all, Stalin was wary of people committed to staying poor, like Bukharin. He did not understand their motives" (p. 105).

Stalin sees and punishes shortcomings in everyone: in the people at large, in the East European Party chieftains, in the Old Bolsheviks, in Lenin himself. He even admits some of his own weaknesses and errors; for running away from Moscow in October 1941, when the Nazis were at the gates of the capital, "he punished himself, too— he stood in review at the November military parade. This moment in his life was like the time he had fallen into an ice hole during his exile in Turukhansk: ice and despair, but out of ice and despair had come strength. It was no laughing matter—a military parade with the enemy at the walls" (p. 90). But for others, the punishment is more dire: death. Socialism cannot be built without Stalin, nor in any other way than Stalin has built it—and now the upstart Tito has dared to say there is another way.

[8] Pp. 100–101. This is one example of Solzhenitsyn's deliberately symbolic use of names. See below.

The years 1936 and 1937 had been so glorious! So many heads hitherto untouched had fallen that year, but he had let Tito slip out of his hands. . . . Like a legendary hero, Stalin had all his life been cutting off the hydra's ever-sprouting heads. He had disposed of a whole mountain of enemies in his lifetime. And he had tripped on a root.

Iosif had tripped over Iosif.[9]

Now Stalin is profoundly concerned: "How could he leave humanity? In whose care? They'd make a mess of everything." [10]

Solzhenitsyn is obsessed by the official use of the classical Potemkin façade; he wishes to tear the mask off the face of Soviet life so that its citizens can discern the features beneath. It is a gargantuan task, Tolstoyan in conception, and requires novelistic gifts of the first order, for everywhere Solzhenitsyn sees façade and falsehood covering reality and truth—in the notions of the state, the church, the people, and history. From the very opening scene of the novel, Solzhenitsyn exploits this tension be-

[9] P. 91. *Iosif* Stalin had tripped over *Iosif Broz*, i.e., Tito.
[10] P. 113. It is worth comparing Solzhenitsyn's portrait of Stalin with two others, nonfiction, that by his daughter, Svetlana Alliluyeva, in *Twenty Letters to a Friend* (1967) and Milovan Djilas' *Conversations with Stalin* (1962), and one other fictional one, by Igor Gouzenko in *The Fall of a Titan* (1954). Given some differences because of the time at which they are portraying Stalin, Solzhenitsyn's depiction is similar to theirs in general outline, but the others are richer and more complex, less monolithic and more human.

tween illusion and reality, stressing it with irony, humor, and bitterness. Volodin, though a Foreign Ministry official and a member of the ruling first circle, behaves like a decent human being but must call Dobroumov anonymously from a public telephone booth, disguising his natural voice. In the second scene, the "golden cage" of the *sharashka* is a hell and a prison, but the zeks coming from the concentration camps think it is heaven, for Mavrino has plenty of food, warmth, cigarettes, and even private toilet facilities instead of buckets in a cell. The Mavrino zeks greet them with the comment that because the concentration camps are given poetic names, "You'd think there was some great unrecognized Pushkin in the MVD. He doesn't bother about long poems or even verses; he just gives poetic names to concentration camps" (pp. 6–7). There is other such conversational interplay: Pryanchikov acidly asks Lev Rubin, who still considers himself a Communist though he has been imprisoned in the *sharashka*, how human beings can be numbered, "is that what you call progressive?" Another Mavrino zek, Potapov, who helped design and build the Dnieper dam, tells how the Russians imprisoned him for having sold the dam to the Germans—*after* the dam had been blown up. In the third scene, Rubin, the Communist stalwart, is celebrating Christmas with five German prisoner-of-war technicians who are also working at Mavrino. A philologist specializing in Germanic languages, Rubin had been part of a Soviet psychological-warfare team during the war and had been arrested by the Soviet political police after the war, despite his wartime bravery and accomplishments, because he had agitated against a postwar policy of blood, death, and revenge against the Germans. Rubin is still trying to propagandize the Germans—after all he remains a Communist—and gives them a highly slanted and censored version of the news, because he cannot bear to explain "that in our complex age Socialist truth sometimes progresses in a roundabout, distorted way" (p. 12). But one of the Germans has built a tiny radio receiver and has listened to BBC in German and knows that what Rubin is telling them is a lie; he has also told his fellow Germans, but none of them mentions this to Rubin.

All the so-called free employees at the *sharashka* are MGB (Ministry of State Security) officers, and themselves prisoners. The MGB officers are all warned, during their indoctrination, that the prisoners they must deal with have their own Potemkin façades, so these prisoner "dregs of the human race, people unworthy of speaking the Russian language . . . were particularly dangerous because they did not openly show their wolf fangs but constantly wore a mask of courtesy and good breeding" (p. 25). Every one of the twenty-two women who were free (MGB) employees, however, "had either found a secret attachment here [among the zeks], were in love . . . , or had taken pity on someone and put him in touch with his family" (p. 199).

On the rare occasions when zeks are permitted visits by relatives, the zeks are not only taken to other prisons in Moscow to meet their families, but they are issued

"masquerade" clothes: "The prison administration compelled them to change into ordinary clothes for visits, issuing them used suits and shirts which had probably been
confiscated from the private wardrobes of people whose
property had been seized after they were sentenced. . . .
They didn't want the prisoners' relatives to get a bad
impression of prison" (p. 165). But they do not issue the
prisoners shoes for these visits, because the feet are hidden
from the visitors' view.

The two most biting and imaginatively brilliant uses of
the Potemkin façade,[11] of the tension between deliberately
cultivated illusion and deliberately ignored reality, are in
two sections which deal respectively with Russian ancient
and modern history. The first is the account of a mock
trial, conducted by Lev Rubin, of the traditional Russian
hero Prince Igor (as he appears in the Borodin opera and
the early anonymous *Lay of Prince Igor*) [12] according to

[11] Solzhenitsyn has one of the most recalcitrant and independent
zeks, Khorobrov, reading a new novel, a hit, entitled *Far from Us*.
"The book," Solzhenitsyn writes, "was a meat pie without the
meat, an egg with its insides sucked out, a stuffed bird. It talked
about a construction project which had actually been carried out
by zeks, and about camps, but nowhere were the camps named,
nor did it say that the workers were zeks. . . . Instead, they were
changed into Komsomols who were well dressed, well shod, and
full of enthusiasm" (p. 67). Solzhenitsyn is apparently referring to
Anatoly Kuznetsov's novel, *The Continuation of a Legend*,
Yunost, 1957, which Kuznetsov disavowed after his defection in
England.
[12] See Vladimir Nabokov's translation, *The Song of Igor's
Campaign* (New York: Vintage Books, 1960).

present-day Soviet law as a "long-time Polovtsian agent and spy."

> Olgovich, Igor Svyatoslavich, born 1151, a native of the city of Kiev, of Russian nationality, non-Party, previously unconvicted, a citizen of the U.S.S.R., by profession a military leader, serving in the position of troop commander with the rank of prince . . . is accused of the following:
> "That he willfully executed vile treason against his country, combined with sabotage, espionage, and collaboration over a period of many years with the Polovtsian Khanate. . . ." [p. 303]

Rubin goes on, to the entertainment of the zeks for whom he is performing, to indict official Soviet assumptions that no wounded man should permit himself to be taken prisoner on the battlefield, that marriage to foreigners is a crime, that escape from captivity and voluntary return to one's homeland is not believable and therefore a crime; since Prince Igor has done all of these things, "there can be one and only one interpretation: Prince Igor was recruited by Polovtsian intelligence and sent back to assist in the distintegration of the Kievan state!" (pp. 305–306).

An even bitterer mockery of Soviet justice—and of Western naïveté—is contained in the chapter entitled "Buddha's Smile." The chapter tells a story concocted by Nerzhin and Potapov when they were in Butyrskaya Prison in the summer of 1946, and is obviously based on

77

Mrs. Franklin Delano Roosevelt's visit to that Soviet prison after the war, when she was investigating the use of UNRRA aid in the Soviet Union.[13] She asked to see a prison and was taken to the Butyrskaya. But in the novel, before the character Mrs. R—— arrives there, the prisoners of Cell 72 create a new Potemkin village for her—with the help of their jailers of course. The MVD officials take the zeks out of their cell and have them bathed, barbered, perfumed, and put into new clothes. Their cell is repainted and carpeted, the windows fixed to permit fresh air to circulate, and a guard especially stationed in the courtyard with an adjustable mirror to direct sunshine into the cell so that it will seem to be sunny all the time. There are new cots, white sheets, night tables, books, and cigarettes —though the zeks are forbidden to touch the cigarettes because they have been provided personally by the prison chief rather than by the MVD budget—and even copies of *Amerika* magazine. An icon lamp is set in a niche before an icon of the Virgin Mary with the Child, and copies of the Bible, the Koran, and the Talmud are left

[13] "The widow of the well-known statesman, a perspicacious woman prominent in many good causes, who had done much to defend the rights of man, Mrs. R—— had undertaken the task of visiting America's brilliant ally and seeing with her own eyes how UNRRA aid was being used. Rumors had reached America that UNRRA food was not being distributed to ordinary people. And she also wished to see whether freedom of conscience was being violated in the Soviet Union. She had already been shown ordinary Soviet citizens—officials who had changed out of uniform for the occasion—and in their rude work clothes they thanked the United Nations for its unselfish help" (p. 334).

there—and also a small bronze statute of Buddha smiling. When they bring Mrs. R——, her Soviet guides make it seem as if they pick Cell 72 at random and conduct her and the accompanying Quaker ladies into the cell. The prisoners are diffident. She asks why they're not smoking, and they tell her they're trying to give it up because it's poison—but only after the major-general whose personal cigarettes are there looks askance at one zek who lights up. When Mrs. R—— asks what one of the zeks was convicted for—he actually received a ten-year sentence for a careless acquaintance with an American tourist—she is told that he burned a village, worked for the Gestapo, raped three Russian peasant girls, and killed numberless Russian children. Mrs. R—— wants to know if he has been condemned to death, and the MVD major general blandly explains, "No, we hope he will reform. He has been sentenced to ten years of honest labor." She tells the translators to ask if the prisoners want to complain about anything to the United Nations; the major general warns them in Russian about smoking his cigarettes, threatening them with solitary confinement. The prisoners are quite indignant, and the translator tells Mrs. R——, "They unanimously protest against the serious predicament of Negroes in America and demand that the Negro question be submitted to the United Nations." [14] Mrs. R—— is persuaded that the Butyrskaya is a magnificent prison and is convinced "of

[14] P. 335. Solzhenitsyn's references to America and American aid are uniformly appreciative.

the falsity of the innuendoes spread by hostile people in the West" (p. 336).

The moment she has gone, the prisoners are taken out of the cell, and it and they are restored to their original dilapidated and deprived condition. One zek, found with the Sermon on the Mount inside his cheek—he has torn it out of the pocket Bible ostentatiously displayed in the Potemkin cell—is thereupon beaten "first on the right cheek and then on the left" (p. 337).

That Solzhenitsyn's testimony in these matters is intended not simply for his own people, but for the outside world as well, is demonstrated in these bitter black-humor scenes. There are a number which stress the Western failure to perceive and understand Soviet reality, which underline the way in which Western observers are taken in by the Potemkin façade. Perhaps the most important of these is the final scene in the book, always of immense significance in any work of fiction. In what is an extended and ironic double entendre and metaphor of Soviet life, Solzhenitsyn shows Nerzhin being driven from Mavrino to the Moscow railway station where he is to be put on a transport to one of the nefarious Siberian slave-labor camps. He and the other zeks on the transport are driven through the Moscow streets in a closed truck with the words for meat and bread painted on its sides in four languages—Russian, French, German, and English—and it is noticed by the "correspondent of the progressive French paper *Libération.*"

In the final two paragraphs, Solzhenitsyn writes a coda

which echoes the themes of agony explored in the book
and which is intended to reverberate in Western minds for
a long time:

> He [the *Libération* correspondent] remembered
> that he'd already seen more than one such van today,
> in various parts of Moscow. And he took out his
> notebook and wrote in red ink:
> "On the streets of Moscow one often sees vans
> filled with foodstuffs, very neat and hygienically im-
> peccable. One can only conclude that the provision-
> ing of the capital is excellent." [p. 580]

Solzhenitsyn is saying that what on the surface appears
to be progress in Soviet life is, in fact, a disguise for a
police state and a penal colony, for the treatment of
human beings as meat.

Solzhenitsyn lays even more stress on the final scenes
of his novels than most writers do, as both *Ivan Denisovich*
and *Cancer Ward* show. In *Denisovich* the last scene is
meant to sum up the final irony, which is that the single
day that has been shown of Shukhov's sentence was almost a happy day, In the final scene of *Cancer Ward*,
Solzhenitsyn is stressing the essential malignance in human
nature, the "causeless" violence and aggression, while
simultaneously portraying an individual who is striving
against that evil and who may, in fact, have gone a long
way toward overcoming it.

(There are a number of interesting Potemkin-façade
stories about Americans and Russians. The former Ameri-

can Vice-President Henry Wallace visited the notorious Magadan slave-labor camp in 1944 and then wrote admiringly about it in his *Soviet Asia Mission.* Marchenko, in *My Testimony*, reports that U-2 pilot Gary Powers was held in special custody in Vladimir Prison, confined in a carefully provisioned cell, with special food and clothing and even a hand-picked companion, a prisoner from the Baltic countries who had been promised that his twenty-five-year sentence would be canceled if, during Powers' incarceration, the Balt could keep the American flier from learning about Soviet reality. The Balt was enjoined "not to tell Powers about the real situation of the prisoners in Soviet prisons, but on the contrary . . . do everything he could to strengthen the conviction that all political prisoners were kept in the same conditions as they themselves [were, and he] was told to say as little as possible about the ordinary way of life in the Soviet Union." Marchenko remarks: "it was in vain, of course, that some of our prisoners hoped that when he [Powers] was back home, the American flyer would be able to tell them there about our particular circle of hell. Powers was not allowed even a sniff of our real prison life.") [15]

The First Circle is much concerned with the "heirs of Stalin" and "fathers and sons" problems. Solzhenitsyn not only shows Stalin at the apex of the pyramid, in his own topmost "first circle," but shows all the "little Stalins" in the first circles all the way down through the pecking

[15] *My Testimony*, pp. 157–158.

order of Soviet society, from Abakumov at the head of the secret police to the spies at Mavrino who inform on their fellow zeks to the security officers. Each little Stalin is servile to his superiors and brutal to his subordinates. Everywhere there is lust for power and place, ambition and acquisitiveness that brook neither opposition nor compromise and are unrestrained either by law or ethics. Those who rise are the mediocre, ignorant, sycophantic, brutal—those without morals or personal integrity. Solzhenitsyn does not, therefore, lay the blame at Stalin's door alone. Solzhenitsyn's indictment is of all the institutions of the entire society: the government, the Party, the judiciary, the police—particularly the police. Everywhere he portrays a police state in which coercion, blackmail, informing, and violence are the way of life into which people are pressed. But he does not exempt the people from culpability either. Nerzhin, talking to Rubin about Rubin's teaching Russian to the German prisoners of war, acerbly remarks:

> Even nonpolitical Max—doesn't he, too, share some responsibility with the [Nazi] executioners? After all, he didn't do anything to stop them.
> Just as we, right now, are not doing anything to stop Abakumov or Shishkin-Myshkin. [p. 18]

For cooperating with the ruling circle, the heirs of Stalin and their accomplices are rewarded with privileges which make them a distinct "new class"—in the Djilas sense of the term—a powerful and privileged ruling elite.

83

Or, as Solzhenitsyn himself comments: "If a man can buy things in a store other than the store that everyone uses, he will never buy anywhere else. If a person can be treated in a special clinic, he will never be treated anywhere else. If a person can ride in a personally assigned car, he won't think of riding any other way" (p. 232). So long as Innokenty Volodin obeys the orders of the Foreign Ministry, he will be able to live the life of the Soviet version of the privileged "jet set."

> They belonged to that circle of society in which people do not know what it means to walk or take the subway, that group who even before the war preferred planes to sleeping cars, who never even had to concern themselves with furnishing an apartment. Wherever they went—Moscow, Teheran, the Syrian coast, Switzerland—a furnished house, villa, or apartment awaited the young couple. And their philosophies of life were the same: "We have only one life!" So take everything life can give, except one thing: the birth of a child. For a child is an idol who sucks dry the juices of your being without any return for your sacrifices, not even ordinary gratitude. [p. 340]

Volodin's father-in-law, the special prosecutor Major General Pyotr Makarygin, has done so well by the regime that the regime has done almost as well by him: he has an apartment with two bathrooms, two kitchens, five other rooms, two Bashkir maids, silver, china, furniture—and the Order of Lenin.

As a party in the generational conflict that the Soviets call "fathers and sons," Makarygin's youngest daughter, Clara, opposes her father's whole way of life. She criticizes the fact that some live in hovels and others in mansions, that some have chauffeur-driven cars while others walk to work with holes in their shoes. And she enrages him most by saying, "They wouldn't be paying you thousands [of rubles] if you weren't giving them something in return!" (p. 367).

What is true of the first circle outside is also true of the first circle inside the penal system. Mavrino not only provides enough food and drink, warmth, tobacco, and relatively meaningful work; it even offers the zek an opportunity to be freed, to have his sentence remitted or to be pardoned, by cooperating with the regime.

> In the sharashkas, those cushiony institutions where the snarl of the camp struggle for existence was not heard, it had long since been the established rule that those zeks most involved in the successful solution of a problem received everything—liberty, a clean passport, an apartment in Moscow; while the rest received nothing, not a single day off their term, nor three ounces of vodka in honor of the victors. [p. 50]

What the ruling circle insists on is compliance and unquestioning obedience in carrying out its injunctions. But noncompliance or what it considers opposition, it punishes harshly. Nerzhin, for example, is offered a new cryptographic group to work with which Colonel Yakonov has organized at Mavrino. If he cooperates, he will be freed, be given an apartment in Moscow, and have the conviction removed from his record. The recalcitrant Nerzhin furiously refuses both his cooperation and their reward: "They'll remove the conviction from my record!" Nerzhin cried angrily. . . . "Where did you get the idea that I want that little gift? . . . You're beginning at the wrong end. Let them admit first that it's not right to put people in prison for their way of thinking, and then *we* will decide whether we will forgive *them*" (p. 43). For this denunciation Nerzhin pays the price: Yakonov marks him for a transport due to leave for the concentration camps in a few days. Another recalcitrant zek, Ilya Khorobrov, refuses to work more than the twelve hours required by the Soviet constitution—and is also put on the same transport for this act of "mutiny."

Everywhere the police insist that compliance be both demeaning and incriminating; those who are "loyal" must become police informers. Not only does this give the political police sources of information, but it gives them a hold on those sources as well. One is called on to denounce one's family and friends, one's colleagues and co-workers. From the top of the society to the bottom one must be an informer or an accomplice to be acceptable to the regime. Muza, one of the students who shares Nerzhin's wife's room in the student quarters, is threatened by two MGB agents and told that unless she becomes a secret informer, they will wreck her university career. All the zeks are aware that many among them are informers. One Isaak Kagan, is a man who "had tried to live an obscure life and pass through the Era of Great Accomplishments sideways" (p. 295), but the secret police had tried to make him an informer. He had refused, and they had convicted him under Article 58, paragraph 12, for *failure to inform,* and sentenced him to ten years' imprisonment; but ironically, in the *sharashka,* he becomes an informer. Pryanchikov, another of the zeks, tells how the close friend with whom he was in a Nazi concentration camp, with whom he ate from the same bowl, and with whom he escaped from the Germans, was the one who eventually betrayed him to the NKVD. Adam Roitman, Yakonov's deputy at the Mavrino *sharashka* and a major in the MGB, is also a gifted scientific researcher and a Stalin Prize winner. He remembers how, as a Young Pioneer of twelve, he was involved in denouncing a fellow student for anti-Semitism and for having an "alien class origin." After that student, Oleg, insisted that "every person has the right to say anything he thinks," and went to school with a cross hanging from a chain around his neck and was seen going into church with his mother, a group of "twelve-year-old Robespierres denounced to the student masses the accomplice of anti-Semites and the peddler of religious opium," and Oleg was expelled from both the Pioneers and from school. Though Roitman had not instigated the move, had only been dragged into it, "even now the vileness of it all made him flush with shame" (p. 425).

But perhaps the most painful of the betrayals was by Lev Rubin, that convinced Communist, who betrayed his

own family because of his convictions. Rubin told "when
and where his cousin had belonged to the opposition organization, and what he had done" (p. 413), because the
GPU (political police) man who came to ask him made
clear that he could not refuse to tell the Party. Rubin was a
young man then, and now, middle-aged, when Major
Myshin tries to recruit him as a secret informer, Rubin
refuses. The dialogue between them reveals the regime's
basic psychology in these matters. Myshin says:

> "If you are a Soviet [man], then you will help us.
> "If you don't help us, then you are not a Soviet
> [man].
> "If you are not a Soviet [man], then you are anti-
> Soviet and deserve an additional term."

When Rubin sardonically asks how he is to write his denunciations, in pencil or ink, the Major tells him that
ink would be better, and Rubin replies bitterly, "You see,
I have already proved my devotion to Soviet authority
in blood, and I don't need to demonstrate it in ink" (p.
144).

In Lev Rubin, Solzhenitsyn attempts to portray a decent
and idealistic Communist intellectual, but Rubin, for all
his great learning and intelligence, seems somehow obtuse,
even morally defective, not only because he is able to
betray his cousin to the secret police "for the Party," but
because he is able years later, while working at identifying
the voice tapes of those in the Foreign Ministry who
might have made the telephone call to Dr. Dobroumov,

to cause the arrest of still another man. In doing so, despite all his attempts at logically justifying his actions, he seems both craven and hypocritical, though doubtless Solzhenitsyn is truly portraying the mentality of many such intellectuals in the Soviet Union. Rubin likes the "reckless fellow" who warned Dobroumov, but he is convinced that "objectively that man who had wanted to do what seemed to him the right thing had in fact attacked the positive forces of history. Given the fact that priority in scientific discovery was recognized as important and necessary for strengthening the state, whoever undermined it stood objectively in the way of progress. And had to be swept away" (p. 196). Though Rubin detests the people who give him the task of identifying Volodin, they *objectively* represent the "positive forces" of history, so he must rise above his personal feelings and his own fate to help them find the man and make another victim. Rubin manages to rationalize his own complicity in another, and fascinating, way. When the MVD's General Oskolupov impatiently calls for arresting all the suspects instead of trying to identify the single culprit from the tapes, Rubin is able to reassure himself that "the speed of Oskolupov's decision proved that all the men would have been arrested without Rubin's complicity and without phonoscopy [the method of identifying the voice prints]. So, in fact, he had saved three men" (p. 508).

If there are many willing to be accomplices or coerced into complicity, a few refuse adamantly either to compromise with the regime or to be compromised by it.

Squaring the Circle

When Oskolupov and Yakonov call the zek Gerasimovich in to ask him to invent an infrared camera with which the police can take pictures at night, and tell him that if he suceeds he will be set free, Gerasimovich refuses. In doing so, he not only endangers his own life, but very likely dooms his wife, who cannot go on living without him, yet he tells Oskolupov quietly: "Putting people in prison is not my field! I don't set traps for human beings! It's bad enough that they put *us* in prison" (p. 500). The brilliant scientist Bobynin, when he is called to the offices of Abakumov to inform the Minister of State Security, behind the backs of his "free" bosses, Yakonov and Oskolupov, of the progress of the research, tells Abakumov off curtly, "You need me and I don't need you," and explains why:

> I have nothing, you understand—not a thing! You can't get your hands on my wife and child—a bomb got them first. My parents are already dead. My entire property on earth is my handkerchief; my coveralls and my underwear that has no buttons . . . are government issue. You took my freedom away long ago, and you don't have the power to return it because you don't have it yourself. I am forty-two years old, and you've dished me out a twenty-five-year term. I've already been at hard labor, gone around with a number on, in handcuffs, with police dogs, and in a strict-regime work brigade. What else is there you can threaten me with? What can you

deprive me of? My work as an engineer? You'll
lose more than I will. . . .

. . . Just understand one thing and pass it along to
anyone at the top who still doesn't know that you
are strong only as long as you don't deprive people
of *everything*. For a person you've taken *everything*
from is no longer in your power. He's free all over
again. [p. 83]

Solzhenitsyn sympathizes with those who are crushed or
warped by the regime, approves of those—like Sologdin
—who outwit the regime, but those he admires and loves
are those who resist the regime on principle, who deny it
their cooperation, who are willing to risk torture, the
camps, even death for principle or their own integrity.
Of Bobynin, therefore, he writes (in his own voice),
"One can build the Empire State Building, discipline
the Prussian Army, elevate the state hierarchy above the
throne of the Almighty, but one cannot get past the un-
accountable spiritual superiority of certain people" (p.
52). To the Nerzhins, the Bobynins, the Gerasimoviches,
and the Spiridons, the people who do not betray others or
themselves, Solzhenitsyn gives the laurel, even though he
knows that true as Bobynin's acid comments to Abakumov
are, there is still another truth even beyond:

Unfortunately for people—and fortunately for their
rulers—a human being is so constituted that as long
as he lives there is always something more that can
be taken away from him. Even a person imprisoned

for life, deprived of movement, of the sky, of family, of property, can, for instance, be transferred to a damp punishment cell, deprived of hot food, beaten with clubs, and he will feel these petty extra punishments as intensely as his earlier downfall from the heights of freedom and affluence. To avoid these final torments, the prisoner follows obediently the humiliating and hateful prison regime, which slowly kills the human being within him. [pp. 547–548]

Of all those in the *sharashka*, Solzhenitsyn's protagonist, Gleb Nerzhin, is most drawn to Lev Rubin and to Spiridon, who, with Dmitri Sologdin, exemplify the possible courses of action open to him and, by implication, to all Russians.

Lev Rubin is the idealistic Party member convinced that despite Stalin's "mistakes" and "distortions," Soviet society is moving in the right direction. Nerzhin, in fact, accuses Rubin of being the only one of the zeks who "thinks the Plowman [Stalin] is right, that his methods are normal and necessary." [16] Rubin's basic faith in and apolo-

[16] P. 35. Rubin lauds Stalin as a combination of Robespierre and Napoleon and says that Nerzhin cannot understand Stalin or any contemporary history because he is a mere mathematician. Nerzhin counters with the comment that the people who discovered the neutrino and weighed Beta Sirius are not so infantile that they "can't orient themselves in the simple problems of human existence." Soviet historians "don't write history; they just lick a certain well-known spot. So . . . the scientific intelligentsia . . . have to study history" themselves (p. 36). This is a view which underlies a good deal of such scientific dissidence as Andrei Sakharov's.

gia for the Party, for Stalin and the heirs of Stalin, and for "socialism" are identical with those being offered by the Party-line intellectuals: The Soviet Union succeeded in industrializing and collectivizing; the Soviet people turned back the Nazis and went all the way to Berlin; the country then succeeded in repairing its war damage and in continuing its industrialization; therefore, the Party and the leadership were "right." Rubin has, however, come to realize that in spite of these achievements, the foundations of moral behavior in the Soviet Union have been seriously eroded, "especially among the younger generation; people [have] lost their feeling for beautiful moral action" (p. 416). He begins to wonder if perhaps it is not more important to improve public morality in the country than to build the Volga-Don Canal or Angaras-troi. To restore moral sensibility, Rubin is writing a proposal for consideration by the Party Central Committee which calls for creating a series of "civic temples" through whose ritual observances public morals and public taste would be developed. The key to success in the project would be the "temple attendants," who must enjoy the "love and trust of the people because of their own irre-proachable, unselfish, and worthy lives" (p. 417). What Rubin is calling for is a kind of "socialism with a human face," and also a new kind of Communist Party, in which all members will be morally upright and full of socialist humaneness and idealism.

Because Rubin is committed to Marxist-Leninist notions of class conflict and to the virtues of the "dictatorship of the proletariat," he is constrained to believe that "to look for life's loftiest meaning in the peasant class was a squalid and fruitless occupation, because only the proletariat was consistently purposeful to the end, and to it alone the future belonged. Only through the collectivism and unselfishness of the proletariat could life achieve its highest significance" (pp. 386–387).

Rubin, however, is a Communist and therefore a member of a minority—is this one reason why Solzhenitsyn makes him a Jew?—and he is portrayed, not only as having betrayed his own cousin to the GPU, but also as having worked with Party ruthlessness in the collectivization program, pitiless in the face of starving and dying kulaks. Since then, however, Rubin has felt that his war wounds, his physical ailments, and his imprisonments are all part of the retribution for his behavior during that harrowing task. Yet he remains a convinced Communist, loyal to the Party and its imperatives.

Sologdin, on the other hand, is equally certain that he has the absolute truth in his hands. He "knew equally well that 'the people' is an over-all term for a totality of persons of slight interest, gray, crude, preoccupied in their unenlightened way with daily existence. Their multitudes do not constitute the foundation of the colossus of the human spirit. Only unique personalities, shining and separate, like singing stars strewn through the dark heaven of existence, carry within them supreme understanding" (p. 387). If Rubin, out of loyalty to Communism, has betrayed his own family, oppressed the peasants, and is now cooperating with the very political police who imprisoned him in trapping and imprisoning Innokenty Volodin, Solzhenitsyn creates Sologdin as a man who looks out only for himself. Hardened and embittered by his experiences in having had his wife denounce him and stop writing to him after he was imprisoned, never having seen the son she was pregnant with when he was arrested, Sologdin has managed to survive the forests of Cherdynsk, the Vorkuta mines, and two secret-police interrogations, one lasting a year, the other six months. Now, having analyzed the system, he coldly and shrewdly plots to obtain his own freedom, proud that his intellect has endured malnutrition and deprivation and still remained creative. Sologdin has invented an absolute coding device which is just what Yakonov needs. Yakonov, by chance, sees the sketch of it on the desk of Professor Chelnov— the brilliant mathematician who once called Stalin a loathsome reptile and who is consequently in his eighteenth year of imprisonment without a verdict, sentence, or hope —the only person at Mavrino to whom Sologdin has confided his theory. Yakonov immediately calls Sologdin to his office to ask about the sketch, but Sologdin, having been told by Chelnov that Yakonov has seen and grasped the implications of the sketch, deliberately burns the only copy before he goes to the Colonel's office.

In a brilliantly rendered scene in which Yakonov's desperation to acquire such an encoder is balanced against Sologdin's desperation not to be cheated either out of his creation or his reward for it, Solzhenitsyn shows how two fundamentally decent men have been corrupted by the system and simultaneously shows how one can deal effectively with both Party and police, by resorting to what they understand and respect: extortion. Sologdin, who heretofore has carefully avoided the attention of the authorities and spurned their favors, now tells Yakonov that the sketch has been burned. Yakonov points out of his office window to the bus stop, from which it is only a half hour's ride to the center of Moscow, and tells Sologdin that if he had not burned that sketch, in six months he would have been getting on that bus himself. Why, the Colonel wants to know, did Sologdin do it? Sologdin realistically explains:

> If I had not burned my drawing, if I had put it in front of you all complete, then our lieutenant colonel, you, Oskolupov, whoever cared to, could have shoved me off on a transport tomorrow and signed any name at all to the drawing. These things have happened. And I can tell you, it's quite inconvenient to complain from a transit camp; they take your pencil away, they don't give you any paper, petitions are not sent on. [p. 459]

Fascinated and delighted by the cool and shrewd manipulations of this zek, Yakonov agrees to Sologdin's demand that the minister or deputy minister be informed that Sologdin is working on the device, that it is his creation, in short, and that either the minister or the deputy sign a personal order naming Sologdin chief designer. With such guarantees, Sologdin promises to reconstruct the absolute encoder within a month so that Yakonov will be saved from Abakumov's punishment, and Abakumov, in turn, will be rescued from Stalin's wrath.

In the contrast and quarrel between Rubin (the bushy black beard) and Sologdin (the precise blond goatee), their differences ultimately are reduced to the essential issue of ends and means. Rubin admits that he does not believe that the ends justify the means for himself, personally, but "it's different in a social sense. Our [Communist] ends are the first in all human history which are so lofty that we can say they justify the means by which they've been attained." Furiously, Sologdin replies that the higher the ends, the higher the means must be— "Dishonest means destroy the ends themselves"—and, further, what applies to the individual must also apply to the masses: "Morality shouldn't lose its force as it increases its scope! That would mean that it's villainy if you personally kill or betray someone; but if the One-and-Only and Infallible [Stalin] knocks off five or ten million, then that's according to natural law and must be appraised in a progressive sense" (p. 404).

Nerzhin rejects both their viewpoints, mass-proletarian (Communist) and individual elitist (capitalist). Among other things, Nerzhin is unable to accept Stalinist collectivization, and in the secret history which he is writing and ultimately must burn and flush down the toilet when Yakonov sends him off to the camps, Nerzhin notes:

I remember a passage in Marx (if I could only find it) where he says that perhaps the victorious proletariat can get along without expropriating the prosperous peasants. That means he saw some economic way of including *all* the peasants in the new social system. The Plowman, of course, did not seek such paths in 1929. And when did he ever seek anything worthwhile or intelligent? Why should a butcher try to be a therapist? [p. 22]

Rubin and Sologdin, who dislike each other, are fond of Nerzhin, yet deride him for his friendship with the peasant Spiridon, calling it a mockery of the "going to the people" of the nineteenth-century *Narodnaya volya* (People's Will) revolutionaries.[17] Nerzhin is, nonetheless, not put off. During the war he learned that he could not ride, harness a horse, pitch hay, or hammer a nail, and ordinary peasant soldiers derided him because of it. When he was arrested, he also saw the elite fail in strength of character and loyalty:

[17] *The Narodnaya volya*, or People's Will, was a nineteenth-century group of populist reformers and revolutionaries who hoped to oust the Tsar and establish a democratic republic based on the "people's will," a will they saw embodied in the Russian peasantry. In an interesting comparison of Sologdin and Spiridon, Solzhenitsyn comments: "Each of them savored his clear superiority over the other—Sologdin because he knew theoretical mechanics, the resistance of materials, and many other scientific matters; Spiridon because all material things were obedient to him. But Sologdin did not conceal his condescension toward the janitor. Spiridon hid his for the engineer" (p. 133).

These delicate, sensitive, highly educated persons who valued beauty often turned out to be cowards, quick to cave in, adroit in excusing their own vileness. They soon degenerated into traitors, beggars, and hypocrites. And Nerzhin had just barely escaped becoming like them. . . . He began to ridicule and mock what he had once worshiped. He strove for simplicity, to rid himself of the intelligentsia's habits of extreme politeness and intellectual extravagance. In a time of hopeless failure, amid the wreckage of his shattered life, Nerzhin believed that the only people who mattered were those who planed wood, worked metal, plowed land, and cast iron with their own hands. He tried to acquire from simple working people the wisdom of capable hands and their philosophy of life. And so he came full circle back to the fashion of the previous century: the creed that one must "go to the people." [p. 388]

Nerzhin had not gone to the people as the nineteenth-century Russian aristocrats had, from above—*noblesse oblige;* he had been thrown among them, an equal among equals, and had learned that the "people" also failed to provide him with models he could follow.

It turned out that the People had no homespun superiority to him. . . . these people were of no greater stature than he. They did not endure hunger and thirst any more stoically. They were no more firm of spirit as they faced the stone wall of a ten-year term. They were no more foresighted or adroit than he during the difficult moments of transports and body searches. They were blinder and more trusting about informers. They were more prone to believe the crude deception of the bosses. . . . And they were also greedier for petty things. . . .

What was lacking in most of them was that personal *point of view* which becomes more precious than life itself.

There was only one thing for Nerzhin to do—be himself. . . .

Everyone forges his inner self year after year.

One must try to temper, to cut, to polish one's soul so as to become *a human being*.

And thereby become a tiny particle of one's own people. [pp. 388–389]

Solzhenitsyn includes in the panorama of the life histories of various members of the intelligentsia in Mavrino the contrasting tale of the fifty-year-old Spiridon Yegorov, the peasant janitor of the *sharashka*—and it is far and away the most moving and encompassing life history of all. The literary son of Matryona and brother of Ivan Denisovich Shukhov, Spiridon is the innocent Ivan who stands for what Solzhenitsyn believes is best in the Russian people.

Symbolically, Spiridon Yegorov was born at the turn of the century; therefore, he was seventeen when the Bolshevik Revolution took place and just over forty when World War II began. The account of the heartbreaking hegira of Spiridon and his family is not only a literary tour de force in which the history of the ordinary peasant in Russia during the three decades between the October Revolution and 1949 is telescoped; it is also a profoundly moving human story. Spiridon endures it all: the Civil War, the NEP (New Economic Policy), the "dekulakization," prison, World War II, capture by the Nazis, escape, partisan warfare against the Germans, recapture by the Germans, shipment to the Reich as a slave laborer, liberation by the Americans, return to the Soviet Union to be imprisoned once more. In that process Spiridon loses his land; his family is scattered and demoralized, his wife, daughter, and sons in labor camps; he loses most of his eyesight and is now virtually blind. Yet the blind Spiridon, uneducated, has insight and behaves with courage, common sense, dignity, and sobriety.

Not one of the eternal questions about the validity of our sensory perceptions and the inadequacy of our knowledge of our inner lives tormented Spiridon. He knew unshakably what he saw, heard, smelled, and understood.

In the same way, everything about his concept of virtue fitted together without forcing. He did not slander anyone. He never lied about anyone. He used profanity only when it was necessary. He killed only in war. He fought only because of his fiancée. He would not steal a rag or crumb from anyone. And if, before his marriage, he had . . . "played around with the skirts," well, had not the supreme authority, Aleksandr Pushkin, confessed that "Thou shalt not covet thy neighbor's wife" was particularly hard on him? . . .

What Spiridon loved was the land.

What Spiridon had was a family.

The concepts of "country" and "religion" and "socialism," which seldom turn up in everyday conversation, were evidently unknown to Spiridon. His ears were closed to them; his tongue would not speak them.

His country was—family.

His religion was—family.

Socialism was—family. [pp. 396–397]

Fascinated by Spiridon, full of admiration for him, Nerzhin is intent on searching out the standards by which the peasant lives, how he distinguishes between right and wrong. When he asks Spiridon, Spiridon replies simply, "The wolfhound is right and the cannibal is wrong!" (p. 401). Though Nerzhin is struck by the simplicity and profundity of the reply, he offers no elucidation of precisely what it means—nor does Solzhenitsyn. What Spiridon seems to be saying is that a wolfhound who kills wolves is doing the "right" thing, doing what he "was intended to do"; but a man who turns cannibal and kills and eats his fellow man is doing the "wrong" thing, what he was "intended *not* to do." The statement remains ambiguous, deliberately, I think, for it may also mean that an animal who kills as a result of his own nature is acting "rightly," while an animal who learns to kill is "wrong."

If almost all the zeks in Mavrino are innocent of wrongdoing, have not by ordinary civilized standards committed any crimes, then their women—wives, girl friends, daughters—are even less culpable, yet they are punished almost as much, and in some ways more, than their men. In this regard, Solzhenitsyn recounts the agony of Nerzhin's wife and her fate as typical of the way the "ruling circle" treats the wives of political "oppositionists." Because the regime wishes to force these women to denounce their men, the prisoners and their women do everything they can to hide their relationships. To protect her standing at the university, Nerzhin, for instance, writes to his wife only in care of general delivery. But a new police edict insists that prisoners give a list of all their close relatives, with their surnames, given names, patronymics, relationship, places of work, and home addresses; and correspondence and visits will be permitted only with those designated close relatives. Secrecy will therefore cut the thin thread of communication with wife or child or parent; openness will cause them to be denounced to the secret police. By hiding the fact that their relatives are behind bars, the families of prisoners have protected their jobs and housing. Old hardened zeks know that the NKVD files are less correlated than most innocents suppose, and refuse to give the information. Nerzhin has refused to give Nadya's address, and hence she doesn't know that they have been granted a visit together on December 25. By chance, Nadya encounters Lieutenant Colonel Klimentiev, the head of the Mavrino Special Prison (as distinguished from Colonel Yakonov, who is head of the research operations at Mavrino), in the Moscow subway. Klimentiev sees her, recognizes her, and reflects:

> Over her hung the unhappy fate of all the wives of political prisoners—the wives, that is, of *enemies of the people:* no matter to whom they appealed, no matter where they might go, once their unfortunate marriages became known, it was as though they dragged behind them their husband's ineffaceable shame. It was as though in everyone's eyes they shared the burden of blame with the black villains to whom they had once carelessly entrusted their fates. And the women began to feel they really were to blame—something that the *enemies of the people* themselves, their husbands, accustomed to their situation, did not feel. [p. 153]

It was not enough for the wife's address to be registered with the MGB. The ministry did its best to see to it that as few wives as possible should yearn to receive those post cards [announcing that they might visit their imprisoned husbands]; that neighbors should be aware of the wives of enemies of the people; that such wives should be brought out in the open, isolated, and surrounded by a healthy public opinion. Which was precisely what the wives were afraid of. [p. 154]

Though Klimentiev considers himself an exemplar of soldierly discipline, he is moved by Nadya's sorrowful mien and her plea that it is an entire year since she has been allowed a visit with Gleb, so he gives her the particulars of the December 25 visit, though that is contrary to regulations he usually follows.

The half-hour meeting between Nerzhin and Nadya, during which no kiss or handclasp is permitted and a guard sits three feet away, watching and listening to every word, is a harrowing and brilliantly written scene. They had been married as students and lived together for only a year before the war separated them. After Nerzhin had been imprisoned, the authorities had not informed Nadya, but simply cut off sending his officer's pension to her. When finally she learned that he had been sentenced to ten years, the news cheered her, because "once again she was not alone on earth. What happiness that it was not fifteen years, not twenty-five years! It is only from the grave that no one returns. People do return from hard labor" (p. 206). Nerzhin then "suddenly understood clearly that Stalin had robbed him and Nadya of their children. Even if his term should end, even if they were together again, his wife would be thirty-six, maybe forty. It would be late for a child" (p. 200). After four years at the front and ten in prison and the prospect of permanent exile thereafter, Nerzhin had realized that there was no way back. Consequently, he had written her early in his imprisonment not to ruin her life but to divorce him and remarry; when she received his letter, she asked him only if he had stopped loving her. Such love fills him with astonishment and admiration, for he recognizes that he himself could not be so unwaveringly faithful even for a year, yet she has already been loyal to him for seven years. Despite his advice to marry again, Nadya has waited for him, has even written: "If any diversions can ease your burden in that hopelessly dismal life—well, what of it? I consent, darling, I even insist—be unfaithful to me, see other women. After all, you will be returning to me, won't you?" (p. 209).

Nadya wants Gleb's advice about the new security questionnaire which has been distributed at the university. If she tells the university authorities her husband is a political prisoner or gives his name—she is using her maiden name and has said that he was killed in the war—they will expel her, not let her defend her dissertation, not give her a job. What she requires from him is his permission and encouragement to disavow him; when she broaches the subject, Gleb notices for the first time that Nadya is no longer wearing his wedding ring. He agrees, encourages her to divorce him, says she should have done so long ago. Nadya leaves, after their precious half hour together, feeling that he is self-sufficient, requires no sympathy, and needs no woman's loyalty; Gleb is left with the sight of her ringless fingers waving goodbye to him. The entire scene between them, in the oppressive and embarrassing circumstances of Lefortovo Prison, is charged with the strain, subdued passion, and awkward intensity of personal experience bitterly and artistically distilled.

In another comparison of the nineteenth and twentieth centuries in Russia, to the detriment of twentieth-century Soviet Russia, Solzhenitsyn records the agonized plaint of Gerasimovich's wife to Nadya while they wait at Lefortovo to see their husbands:

It was easy to love a man in the nineteenth century! The wives of the Decembrists—do you think they performed some kind of heroic feat? Did personnel sections call them in to fill out security questionnaires? Did they have to hide their marriages as if they were a disease? In order to keep their jobs; so that their last five hundred rubles a month wouldn't be taken away from them; so as not to be boycotted in their own apartments; so that when they went to the courtyard to get water people wouldn't hiss at them, calling them "enemies of the people"? Did their own mothers and sisters bring pressure on them to be reasonable and get a divorce? No, on the contrary! They were followed by a murmur of admiration from the cream of society. They graciously presented to poets the legends of their deeds. Leaving for Siberia in their expensive carriages, they did not lose, along with the right to live in Moscow, their last miserable ten square yards; they did not have to think about dealing with such trifles as black marks in their labor booklet, or the pantry where there would be no pots or pans, no black bread! [18]

[18] P. 215. There are many other examples of how the zeks' women are oppressed and persecuted; one of the most depressing and stirr-

Yet, for all Solzhenitsyn's compassion for women and their suffering, for all his skill in characterizing them, for all his genuine admiration for women's personal and ethical "superiority," he reveals a curious detachment in his estimate of them. They seem somehow less important to men than political or moral commitments, less meaningful than work or war, reflection or dispute; their company seems less fulfilling than male comradeship. Even such highly intelligent and intellectual women as Nadya, her roommates, and Clara Makarygin seem removed from significant ideas, important decisions, and crucial events except insofar as they suffer with or succor their men; the women of the zeks are destroyed by their men's convictions—in both senses—and that seems to be all.

For the protagonist, Nerzhin, the passion to understand his world takes precedence over his love for his wife and his concern for her welfare. Nerzhin's love for Nadya seems "fated, predestined to be trampled" (p. 156), and Nerzhin, even in prison, is secretly happy in his unhappiness, because "from his youth on, Gleb Nerzhin had dreaded more than anything else wallowing in daily living. As the proverb says: *'It's not the sea that drowns you, it's the puddle'*" (p. 157). Prison provides not only the opportunity to figure things out, but also the opportunity to find himself, to hone his own character to the cutting edge. And that passion to figure things out "left [him] with

---

ing examples is that of the wife of Ivan Dyrsin, whose letters to him are absolutely scarifying. See pp. 471–476, *The First Circle*, a chapter ironically titled "Indoctrination in Optimism."

neither his work, nor time, nor life—nor his wife. Once a single great passion occupies the soul, it displaces everything else. There is no room in us for two passions" (p. 204). Almost all the men in the book sacrifice their women with varying degrees of "willingness." Nerzhin sacrifices Nadya for his principles and his sense of integrity; Innokenty Volovdin sacrifices Dotnara in order to warn Dr. Dobroumov of the impending plot; Ruska Doronin sacrifices Clara in his trick role as double agent trying to flush out various spies among the zeks at Mavrino; Gerasimovich sacrifices his wife by refusing to cooperate with the authorities; and even Colonel Yakonov has sacrificed the one woman he has most loved—Agniya—in order to further his career. Only Spiridon does not willingly sacrifice his wife and daughter.

Some of the characters pursue their careers with greater caution or deliberate compromise because they are reluctant to sacrifice their families to the imperatives of the regime. In this respect one of the most moving stories in the novel is that of Yakonov, the colonel in charge of research, when he was still a young engineer. At that point, in 1927, he fell in love with the fine, ethereal, contradictory, ascetic, and idealistic Agniya. Yakonov, because of his own class background, knew that if he was to "succeed," he must attach himself to the new society as early and as effectively as possible; but he loved Agniya for her character, although he was not greatly drawn to her physically. Agniya came from a family which had always helped and sided with the persecuted. Her grandmother, mother and aunt had helped the People's Will revolutionaries, her daughters had given refuge to Social Revolutionaries and Social Democrats, and Agniya "was always on the side of the rabbit that was being hunted, of the horse that was being whipped. As she grew up, this came to mean, to the surprise of her elders, that she was for the church because it was supposedly being persecuted." [19] Yakonov tried to persuade Agniya that her sympathy for the church was rooted in her "indifference to life," and that the future belonged to the Bolsheviks with whom he had already allied himself. The church, he maintained, persecuted other people for ten centuries and survived only by its servility to the Tatar invaders:

> Our church lasted because after the invasion Metropolitan Cyril, before any other Russian, went and bowed down before the Khan and requested protection for the clergy. It was with the Tatar sword that the Russian clergy protected its lands, its serfs, and its religious services! And, in fact, Metropolitan Cyril was right, he was a realist in politics. That's just what he should have done. That's the only way to win. [p. 127]

Moreover, Yakonov insisted, the Bolsheviks were for a society without privilege or advantage in status or income, a society devoted to "universal, complete, absolute equality" (p. 127), and what could be better than that?

[19] P. 126. The "supposedly" is here because the account is being given from Yakonov's viewpoint.

Agniya assured Yakonov that he would one day have fame, success, and prosperity. "But *will you be happy, Anton?*" she asked him. After he returned from his trip abroad and wrote the article denigrating foreign science which "was not the complete truth, but . . . was not exactly a lie either," Agniya returned his engagement ring with a little piece of paper on which was written, "For the Metropolitan Cyril" (p. 129). That was the end of their affair. Yakonov was relieved.

But years later, having been demeaned by Abakumov, he remembers Agniya and the day she took him into the church of St. John the Baptist in Moscow; there, Yakonov "for the first time . . . understood the ecstacy and poetry of the prayer" (p. 129). He realizes, two decades later, that he has fulfilled Agniya's prophecy: he is at the peak of his power, he is a colonel in the MVD, he is talented and intelligent and known to be, he has a loving wife and two children, a fine apartment, an automobile, and yet "he did not want to live any longer. Everything was so hopeless within him that he had no strength to move" (p. 130). He married late, after he had been imprisoned in a *sharashka*, one of the very first; his childen are still small, and his wife is "all the dearer to him because he had married her so late in life." He now realizes that Agniya was right, for he has been demeaned, even punched in the nose by Abakumov, and endured it because of these "three human beings with whom he spent no more than one hour a day, but on whose account he squirmed and struggled and played the dictator during all the rest of his waking hours" (p. 119).

Squaring the Circle

The First Circle continues Solzhenitsyn's preoccupations with a number of themes introduced in *Ivan Denisovich*. Something in Christianity, in religion, continues to attract him both ethically and aesthetically, although he does not seem to be moved by profoundly religious belief or by any special fealty to the church; and he has Yakonov ask Agniya if Russia was "ever Christian in its *soul*" (p. 126). The ascetic and equalitarian bent of Solzhenitsyn's temperament is everywhere evident in his distaste for *nouveau riche* ostentation and materialist acquisitiveness, and he has Nerzhin observe: "I personally hold the view that people don't know what they are striving for. They waste themselves in senseless thrashing around for the sake of a handful of goods and die without realizing their spiritual wealth" (p. 34). He stresses the saving grace of work, whether it is the intellectual effort of the zeks in their research or Spiridon sweeping the snow in the courtyard or Rubin, Nerzhin, and Sologdin voluntarily sawing wood for the Mavrino kitchen for the exercise and fresh air and to calm their nerves. Solzhenitsyn indicts the regime and the heirs of Stalin for their unrealistic schedules and schemes, for their paranoid suspicion and constant surveillance, for their corruption and ineptitude, all of which destroy efficiency and the incentives of those who would work. When Bobynin meets Abakumov, he flays the minister relentlessly:

> How do you picture science to yourself? "Oh, wonder-working steed, build me a palace by morning," and by morning there is a palace? . . . Don't you

suppose that in addition to giving orders you need calm, well-nourished, free people to do the work? And without all this atmosphere of suspicion. You know, we were hauling a small lathe from one place to another, and, whether it happened while it was in our hands or later, the bedplate got broken. God only knows why it broke. But it would cost thirty rubles to weld. Yes, and that lathe is a piece of shit, one hundred and fifty years old, with no motor, a pulley under an open belt-drive—and because of that crack Major Shikin, the security officer, has been dragging everyone in and questioning them *for two weeks*, looking for someone to pin a second term for sabotage on. . . . What the hell do you need all these security officers for? After all, everyone says we are working on a secret telephone for Stalin, that Stalin personally is pressing for it. Yet even in an operation like that you can't assure us a supply of material. Either we need condensers we don't have, or the tubes are the wrong kind, or we don't have enough oscillographs. . . . And have you thought about the people? They all work for you twelve, even sixteen hours a day, and you feed only the leading engineers with meat and the rest get bones. Why don't you allow Section 58 [political] prisoners visits with their relatives? We're supposed to have them once a month, and you allow them once a year. Does that help morale? [pp. 84–85]

Solzhenitsyn admires those who risk their comfort and well-being, even their safety and their lives, for principle.

If the process of rising from circle to circle in the Soviet hierarchy is a matter of mediocrity, servility, compromise, Solzhenitsyn prefers the "best" who refuse such methods of rising, who instead take the risks that "don't pay off." This preference is part of Solzhenitsyn's own elitism—and one of the reasons he can make Sologdin's arguments so convincing—a sympathy for those "best" people who suffer most: superior scientists, front-line combat soldiers, Old Bolsheviks, peasants; and these constitute still another "first circle." He has Nerzhin reflect on how the best students among his university classmates have been killed off: "The more talented had been shell-shocked or killed. They were the sort who were always pushing ahead, who didn't stop to look out for themselves. And those from whom nothing could have been expected were now either completing their postgraduate work or already held appointments as lecturers in higher-educational institutions" (p. 41). As Solzhenitsyn writes in his own voice: "Implacably, the eternal law of war functioned: although the people who went to the front went reluctantly, still all the best and most spirited found their way there; and by the same mode of selection most of them perished. The peak of the human spirit and the purity of heroism were [there]" (p. 236).

The same "best and most spirited" were, after the war, found in the camps, and among these Solzhenitsyn limns the courage, dignity, intelligence, and individuality of Nerzhin, of the Dneiperstroi engineer Potapov, who "chose death over well-being" (p. 159), of Gerasimovich, who could not be persuaded to cooperate with the secret police in trapping and arresting other people, of the young rebel Ruska Doronin, who on the "outside" turns into a criminal and on the "inside" turns into a double agent, of Innokenty Volodin, who ultimately chooses to risk his comfort, safety, and entire life to perform an act of decency and descends into the "first circle" of hell that is the Lubyanka. Solzhenitsyn has a special feeling for those who have suffered together, those who are beyond the pale of normal life: prisoners, combat soldiers, Old Bolsheviks, religious believers. One such, the brilliant professor of mathematics Chelnov, represents these figures: for nationality he puts "zek" on his questionnaires instead of "Russian," and declares that only zeks have immortal souls; "free people are often denied one because of the vain lives they lead" (p. 171). Another such is the Captain of Combat Engineers Shchagov, who wishes to seduce Nerzhin's wife. When Muscovites try to patronize him at the university by asking, "What backwater are you from?" Shchagov replies: "You never had the chance to go there. From a province called the Front. A village called Foxhole" (p. 288). Among such beyond-the-pale groups there is a kindred spirit, a sense of community that Solzhenitsyn particularly admires:

> He [Shchagov] could think of people in only one way: either they were soldiers or they were not. Even in the anonymity of the Moscow streets he maintained this distinction: among all human beings,

only soldiers were bound to be sincere and friendly. Experience had taught him not to trust anyone who had not been tried in the fire of war. . . .

When he came back from the war, Shchagov, like many front-liners, was stunned. They returned—for a little while—better people than when they had left. They returned cleansed by the closeness of death, and the change in their country struck them all the harder because of that—a change which had occurred far behind the front lines, a kind of hard-heartedness and bitterness, often a total lack of conscience, a chasm between starving poverty and the insolence of fattening wealth. [pp. 288–289]

This moral superiority and sense of camaraderie characterize all these groups and set them off—against and above Soviet society—in Solzhenitsyn's eyes.

Solzhenitsyn remains obsessed with the role of art in life, with the nature of art, and with the duty of the artist in Soviet society. Just as he included, perhaps unnecessarily, in *One Day in the Life of Ivan Denisovich*, the discussion of Eisenstein's cinematic art, so, too, the role of art and artists in Russian life intrudes into *The First Circle*, though its inclusion here seems considerably less forced. Throughout the novel there are comments on literature, particularly on Soviet literature. Khorobrov notes the falsity and distortion of history in an essay by Alexei Tolstoy—the Non-Tolstoy as he is derisively called in the *sharashka*—in which

Tolstoy, under the date June 1941, has written, "German
soldiers, driven by terror and insanity, ran into a wall of
iron and fire at the border." Khorobrov also remarks on
the general quality of Russian writers who seemed to be
writing not "for people but for simpletons of no experience who, in their feeble-mindedness, were grateful for
any kind of diversion" (p. 167).

> Everything that really tore and shook the human
> heart was absent from their books. If the war had
> not come, all they could have done was to become
> professional eulogists. The war opened the way for
> them to simple, generally comprehensible human feel-
> ings. But here, too, they elevated to Hamlet-like
> heights all sorts of fantastic and impossible conflicts—
> such as the Komsomol member who blew up dozens
> of ammunition trains behind enemy lines but, because
> he wasn't a member in good standing of any Party
> organization, was torn day and night by uncertainty
> whether he was a real Komsomol member if he didn't
> pay dues.
>   . . . In every story there was some obligatory
> abomination about America. Venomously assembled,
> they made up such a nightmarish picture that one
> could only be amazed that the Americans had not yet
> fled the country or hanged themselves. [p. 168]

Instead of reading such trash, the prisoners, who covet
books, prefer to read *The Count of Monte Cristo.*
    In another place, reflecting on the great purges and the

show trials of the Old Bolsheviks, Nerzhin considers the role Russian writers played in creating and buttressing Stalinism: "Russian writers who dared trace their spiritual inheritance from Pushkin and Tolstoi wrote sickly-sweet eulogies of the tyrant. Russian composers, trained in the Herzen Street conservatory, laid their servile hymns at his pedestal" (p. 203). When Clara Makarygin decides to give up the study of literature at the institute, she does so because "at the institute they never mentioned that world, as if they did not even know it existed. They studied a kind of literature which dealt with everything on earth except what one could see with one's own eyes" (p. 237).

At a party given by the Makarygins, Innokenty Volodin's sister-in-law, Dinera, who is married to the writer Nikolai Galakhov,[20] and who is "not tied down by a Party or literary position, attacked harshly, though always just within the bounds. Dramatists, scenario writers, directors— no one was spared, not even her own husband." But she is permitted this kind of "daring," as she is permitted the dar-

---

[20] The character Galakhov seems to be a combination of Nikolai Gribachev and Vsevolod Kochetov, two of the leading dogmatic Soviet writers. *The First Circle* has a *roman à clef* dimension, not easily available to Western readers, which will for a long time pique and intrigue Kremlinologists and literary critics. Not only the literary and artistic references seem to have specific persons in mind, but even the zeks seem to be modeled on living people. For example, Lev Rubin is said to be based on Lev Kopelev, literary critic and friend of Solzhenitsyn, who was a prisoner with the novelist—see Paul Wohl, *Christian Science Monitor*, Nov. 26, 1969—and very likely, in time, the various "prototypes" will emerge, as some already have concerning *Ivan Denisovich*.

ing of her dress and her way of life, and however mildly honest they are, her attacks come as "a breath of fresh air in the vapid atmosphere of literary criticism turned out not by men but by the official positions they occupied." They are discussing the play *Unforgettable 1919*, by Vsevolod Vishnevsky, which shows how "Stalin had saved Petrograd, saved the entire Revolution, saved all Russia. The play, written for the seventieth birthday of the Father and Teacher, revealed how, under Stalin's guidance, Lenin had somehow managed to cope" (p. 349). What enrages Solzhenitsyn is the distortion of life, reality, and history in Soviet writing, the oversimplifications, the dogmatism, the crass propaganda. He is committed to the view which, elsewhere, Nadya's roommate Muza enunciates about the role of Russian writing: "Have you ever noticed what makes Russian literary heroes different from the heroes of Western novels? The heroes of Western literature are always after careers, money, fame. The Russians can get along without food and drink—it's justice and good they're after" (p. 280). At the Makarygin party, Innokenty Volodin, in the throes of his own crisis of conscience about his call to Dobroumov, tries to talk honestly about writing to his Stalin Prize laureate brother-in-law, Galakhov. Gently, he asks:

> Nikolai, does literature really have to repeat the military statutes? Or the newspapers? Or the slogans? Mayakovsky, for instance, considered it an honor to use a newspaper clipping as an epigraph for a poem.

In other words, he considered it an honor not to rise above the newspaper! But then why have literature at all? After all, the writer is a teacher of the people; surely that's what we've always understood? And a great writer—forgive me, perhaps I shouldn't say this, I'll lower my voice—a great writer is, so to speak, a second government. That's why no regime anywhere has ever loved its great writers, only its minor ones. [p. 358]

The two brothers-in-law do not know each other very well and are quite cautious with each other; before they can achieve any truthful exchange at the party, they are interrupted.

But Galakhov knows that it is getting harder and harder for him to write, that he has sold out his talent. He knows himself unable to answer positively the agonizing question Innokenty has asked: "What ideas have you brought to this tortured age of ours? Other than those unquestioned ideas, of course, that Socialist Realism provides for you?" (p. 359). Galakhov knows, too, that though he has fame, immortality has escaped him; his plays, short stories, and novel "had died on their feet before he was thirty-seven." Yet, in some way, he must come to terms with this "denial of immortality," and uncomfortably he rationalizes:

Why should one necessarily seek immortality? Most of Galakhov's colleagues didn't; their present situations were what mattered, how things went for them during their lives. The hell with immortality, they said; isn't it more important to influence the course of events in the present? . . . Their books served the people; were published in huge editions; were supplied by a system of automatic mass distribution to all libraries; and months of promotion were devoted to them. Of course, they couldn't write much of the truth. [p. 360]

At the same party, the young critic Alexei Lansky, who is courting Clara Makarygin, discusses the poverty of the theater with Dinera, Clara's sister. Dinera objects that in all the plays, "you know ahead of time who's good, who's bad, and how it will come out," [21] and asks why playwrights in Soviet Union never worry about how their plays will be received, why they never flop. Lansky "explains": "Plays never fail here, and can't fail, because the playwrights and the public share the same vision, both artistically and in their general view of the world" (p. 350).

In the *sharashka* there is a zek painter, Kondrashev-Ivanov, who has been sentenced to twenty-five years in a labor camp for having attended a literary evening where an unrecognized and unpublished writer had read parts of his novel to a dozen friends. Kondrashev-Ivanov had, instead of going to a labor camp, been sent to Mavrino, where he is "court painter," painting pictures gratis for

[21] P. 350. Lansky explains that in "real" life too there is no "uncertainty": "Do you think that in real life our fathers had any doubt how the Civil War would end? Did we have any doubt how the War of the Fatherland would end, even when the enemy was in the suburbs of Moscow?"

various police officials with which to decorate their apartments. His work norm is one painting a month. He and Nerzhin discuss painting in general, and Kondrashev-Ivanov's in particular. Many people think Kondrashev's paintings too majestic, too exalted, so they believe he is portraying the Caucasus and not Russia, but Kondrashev insists that there are such scenes in Russia, remarking:

> The public has been fooled by [Issak] Levitan [a nineteenth-century painter of melancholy but lyrical landscapes]. After Levitan we've come to think of our Russian nature as low-key, impoverished, pleasant in a modest way. But if that's all our nature is, then tell me where all those rebels in our history come from: the self-immolators, the mutineers, Peter the Great, the Decembrists, the "People's Will" revolutionaries? [p. 256]

Moreover, Kondrashev maintains that those "self-immolators," however many there are, do not surrender their spirits or their consciences to tyranny, not even in the camps. Nerzhin disagrees with him, arguing that "circumstances determine consciousness," but Kondrashev refuses for an instant to accept this. The human spirit rises above circumstances, or else there would be nothing worth living for. People who love each other remain faithful to each other even when they are separated, yet the circumstances dictate that they should betray each other. Kondrashev continues to insist:

A human being . . . possesses from his birth a certain essence, the nucleus, as it were, of this human being. His "I." And it is still uncertain which forms which: whether life forms the man or man, with his strong spirit, forms his life! Because . . . he has something to measure himself against, something he can look to. Because he has in him an image of perfection which in rare moments suddenly emerges before his spiritual gaze.

Nerzhin feels superior to the "fantastic concepts of this ageless idealist," but respects his point of view (p. 257).

In the scene with Kondrashev, Solzhenitsyn—through Nerzhin's eyes—describes two paintings Kondrashev painted "for himself." One of them, "The Maimed Oak," is symbolic of Russia:

It showed a solitary oak which grew with mysterious power on the naked face of a cliff, where a perilous trail wound upward along the crag. What hurricanes had blown here! How they had bent that oak! And the skies behind the tree and all around were eternally storm-swept. These skies could never have known the sun. This stubborn, angular tree with its clawing roots. with its branches broken and twisted, deformed by combat with the tireless winds trying to tear it from the cliff, refused to quit the battle and perilously clung to its place over the abyss. [p. 251]

The second, after which a chapter is named, is called "The Castle of the Holy Grail," and shows a rider on a horse, surrounded by hostile shrubbery in a slumbering primeval forest; he is poised on the lip of an abyss, a deep gorge above which the horse has "just raised its hoof, ready, at the will of his rider, to step back or to hurtle across." The rider, however, is not looking at the abyss but into the distance, where "a reddish-gold light, coming perhaps from the sun, perhaps from something purer than the sun, flooded the sky behind a castle. It stood on the crest of the mountain—which piled up, ledge after ledge—rising in steps and turrets, visible from below the gorge through the ferns and the trees, spiring to the sky, unreal as if woven out of clouds, vibrant, vague yet visible in its unearthly perfection: the aureate-violet castle of the Holy Grail" (p. 258). If the first picture symbolizes Russia, the second symbolizes the Russian artist-intellectual-idealist searching for, striving for, believing in a more perfect society, represented by the castle of the Holy Grail. It is significant that Solzhenitsyn uses the traditional Christian symbol of the Grail and the questing knight, for Solzhenitsyn has Kondrashev painting what the author seems everywhere to be striving for; more than for "socialism with a human face," he seems to be striving for the City of God.

The conflict of generations is especially sharply delineated through the character of Innokenty Volodin, whose father was a Bolshevik hero during the Civil War and died in 1921. Innokenty had always admired his father's struggle "for the ordinary people against the few who lived steeped in luxury" (p. 342), though he now finds himself one of those immersed in "new class" luxury. He had for a long time had contempt for his mother, who was not a Bolshevik and who had not loved his father; but after her death, Innokenty had found her diaries and letters, filled with the love of art and with ethical imperatives of the older, prewar generation. Gradually, Innokenty has come to be torn between his father's revolutionary equalitarianism and his mother's ethical and aesthetic standards; and perhaps he finally comes to telephone Dobroumov because of one of the notations in her diaries: "What is the most precious thing in the world? Not to participate in injustices. They are stronger than you. They have existed in the past and they will exist in the future. But let them not come about through *you*" (p. 343). Up to the time he read those diaries, Innokenty had lived only by the truth that you have but one life; "now he came to sense a new law, in himself and in the world: you also have only one conscience" (p. 345). He knows that Dobroumov will not be the only victim, but Dobroumov is someone he has cherished because the doctor figures in his memories of his mother. (Elsewhere in the novel, Stalin tells Abakumov that they are soon to have a great purge, "the same measures as in 1937," because "before a big war a big purge is necessary."[22] Stalin gives this information to the Minister

---

[22] P. 112. In another context, Solzhenitsyn comments: "It had been two and a half years since the Most Humane of Statesmen had abolished capital punishment for all eternity. But neither the major nor his former informer had any illusions: what could be done with an objectionable person except to shoot him?" (p. 488).

of State Security when Abakumov pleads with Stalin to restore capital punishment.)

But Innokenty has taken the fateful step; in salving his conscience, he has taken the risk that will permit the silent Leviathan to crush him. His voice has been identified by Rubin, and orders for his arrest have been issued. Here, too, the Potemkin façade is part and parcel of the action: Innokenty is duped into believing that his assignment to Paris has been approved, a car is sent for him, and he is taken to the Lubyanka without anyone among his family or friends being apprised. In a chapter appropriately headed by Dante's "Abandon hope, all ye who enter here," Innokenty enters the precincts of hell. In three brilliant and scarifying chapters, Volodin is put into the prison machinery and "processed." The writing is filled with all the heightened sensitivity to detail and psychological foreboding of someone who has experienced such imprisonment himself. Solzhenitsyn shows Volodin's realization that his wife will divorce him and remarry, that his father-in-law will denounce him but his career will nonetheless be blighted, that everyone who knows him will erase him from their memories. He had previously thought that he wouldn't mind dying so much if people knew about it, "if they knew why, and if his death could inspire them" (p. 413). Now he realizes that no one will know and that his death will be useless. Moreover, he had wanted to live to see what the world would be like in the future, a world in which " 'tribal hostilities' would cease. State boundaries would disappear, as well as armies. A world parliament would be convened. They would elect a president of the planet. He would bare his head before mankind and say——" —and then Volodin is interrupted, called for "interrogation" (p. 543). So, in the depths of hell, the Lubyanka abruptly defines good and evil for Innokenty; he gives up the "philosophy of a savage," Epicurus, that what one likes is good, and what one doesn't like is evil: "Stalin enjoyed killing—did that mean that for him killing a virtue? And since being imprisoned for trying to save somebody did not, after all, produce satisfaction, did that mean it was evil?" (p. 553).

What, then, is happiness? Early in the book, in a discussion between Nerzhin and Rubin, Solzhenitsyn has defined it in the terms which Innokenty Volodin eventually is taught by the Lubyanka and the MGB to accept:

> "The transitory nature and unreality of the concept are implicit in the word itself. The word 'happiness' is derived from the word that means this hour, this moment."
> "No, dear Professor, pardon me. . . . 'Happiness' comes from a word that means one's fate, one's lot, what one has managed to hold on to in life. The wisdom of etymology gives us a very mean version of happiness." [p. 31]

And the meaning of life? Nerzhin also remarks: that "We live—that's the meaning. Happiness? When things are going very well, that's happiness, everyone knows that. Thank God for prison! It gave me the chance to think" (p. 33).

As prison has taught Nerzhin, so prison has taught Volodin
—and the same things.

In *The First Circle*, Solzhenitsyn has chosen to write a
novel in the great Russian tradition, a book of Tolstoyan
sweep and scope, with many characters, many levels of
society, many meanings. In many respects, he has succeeded, and where he has failed, he has failed grandly.
Surely and with conviction he has created a moving and
believable metaphor for Soviet society—a place of experiment (the *sharashka*)—and a hell of its own devising (a
police state). Dan Jacobson has remarked that Solzhenitsyn
carefully avoids "the sentimentality of symbolism":

> One can remark on the symbolism of the research
> conducted in the prison on the nature of the human
> voice—that voice which the entire system has as its
> end to stifle—and on the overall ironic pattern of the
> book. Yet, allowing for these, in this book the prison
> remains nothing more or less than a prison, the walls
> around it are real walls and not metaphysical con-
> structs, the sufferings and hopes of the prisoners are
> those of individuals in a particular place at one
> moment in human history. They do not stand for
> anything other than what they are; the author does
> not distract his gaze or ours from them in order to use
> them as illustrations of a larger thesis about life in
> general. It is enough for him that they should be
> what they are.[23]

[23] "The Example of Solzhenitsyn," *Commentary*, May 1969, p.
84.

In fact, however, Solzhenitsyn's intentions are often symbolic and by no means sentimental (nor is symbolism necessarily "sentimental," though it all too often is), and this is especially true of the central device of the novel, the research on, and concern with, the human voice. Not only is the regime's purpose at Mavrino to record and identify the human voice, its purposes are also to learn to scramble and distort it so that it will become altogether unrecognizable and indecipherable. In this not what Soviet propaganda intends to do? Distort Soviet literature and Soviet history (which is another reason for including discussions of such subjects in the novel)? The very language itself? And when distorting the voices fails, are not the camps and the prisons there to stifle them? Solzhenitsyn deliberately chooses to make Nerzhin profoundly concerned with linguistics, Lev Rubin a professional philologist, and Sologdin obsessed with "purifying the language."

Solzhenitsyn is a rare master of the Russian language —not the debased, impenetrably formula-ridden Russian produced by two decades of Stalinist newspapers, schoolbooks and speeches, but the rich mother Russian that calls on all the ancient, all the regional, and all the poetic resources of that difficult, plastic language. Ivan Denisovich's speech is essentially free of foreign-derived words, as is the entire book. One of the prisoner-scientists in *The First Circle* [Sologdin] insists on attempting what he calls "plain speech," in which non-Russian words are banished, even if puzzling archaisms must be substituted. . . . Solzhenitsyn himself has proposed that Russian be purified in this way. His strongly held views on language not only contribute great power and control to his writing but are also typical of other attitudes that pervade his work and his life: he is profoundly attached to all things traditionally Russian, is indeed a patriot of an old-fashioned kind, an instinctive Slavophile who distrusts all things Western.[24]

To assess Solzhenitsyn as a Slavophile in any meaningful sense beyond understanding that the man loves his own language, literature, people, and country is to misconstrue both the man and his work. Nor does he seem to me to distrust all things Western, although he has a healthy skepticism about the essential relevance of Western concepts to Russian reality. But to focus on either of these matters is to miss the point: the point is that in his desire to re-examine the central institutions under which the Russian people live, to reassess Russian history, and to renovate the political and moral life of his country, Solzhenitsyn recognizes that *purification of the language* is essential. Whether he knows Orwell's *Nineteen Eighty-Four* or not, Solzhenitsyn shares Orwell's (and others') concern with the debasement of language and its use in the distortion of truth and history. Not only does Solzhenitsyn insist that the human voice be kept from being stifled—whether by Glavlit or Lubyanka or Vorkuta, not to speak of the grave itself—he insists that the language

[24] "The Writer as Russia's Conscience," *Time*, Sept. 27, 1968, p. 24.

in which the human voice speaks be purified—of Marxist-Leninist jargon, of "socialist realist" strictures, of cant and double-talk and deliberate falsehood. He is genuinely calling for "plain speech," a speech in which in honest language the human voice speaks for the affirmation of moral and humane values.

This same concern for symbolism underlies such large purposes in the novel as the use of "first circle," and such smaller but no less intrinsic intentions as Solzhenitsyn's continual almost playful but usually ironic use of symbolic names for his characters. Sometimes, he deliberately tells the reader he is using such names, as with Poskrebyshev (scraps of dough) in *The First Circle* or Lieutenant Volkovoi (wolf) in *Ivan Denisovich;* sometimes, he lets the reader note them without his help, as with Innokenty (innocent), Spiridon (spirit), Sologdin (loner-individualist), Adamson, the Old Bolshevik (Adam's son; son of the early "pristine" revolutionaries), Satanevich (Satan's son).

It is perhaps in the conflict between realistic achievement and symbolic intention that the gravest shortcomings of the novel are revealed. *The First Circle* does succeed, and brilliantly, in telling how life was lived in the Soviet Union in 1949—and substantially how it is still lived in the same way two decades later; but it fails to transcend the particular circumstances of Soviet society in a way that becomes truly universal and international. Very likely this defect arises from a concatenation of strengths and weaknesses in Solzhenitsyn's own talent, and their inextricable connections are most clearly revealed in the two essential failures of the novel. The first is that Solzhenitsyn fails to give sufficient depth and complexity to the individual human being and so loses the felt life of the unique personal consciousness. So concerned is Solzhenitsyn with depicting the social reality, which he accomplishes brilliantly, that he is much less successful in creating that which he is most committed to defend, the individual, unique human personality. The second shortcoming flows directly from the first. Because character and action are altogether too politicized and submerged in abstract argument and refined polemics about the nature of life, of man, of history, of the state, the narrative itself is diffuse, often slack and sluggish, and sometimes has the quality of journalism rather than of literature. (This journalistic quality is especially evident in the chapters which are concerned with Stalin directly.) In a state which treats, and which Solzhenitsyn flays for treating, human beings almost entirely in political terms, the novelist commits the same error in his novel: his characters are rendered almost entirely on a political plane. Though this is understandable, perhaps even inevitable if one lives in a society so overwhelmingly and nauseatingly politicized and if one chooses, as Solzhenitsyn has, to write a nineteenth-century type of novel set in a political prison, it does, regrettably, reduce the literary and human power of the book.

Yet, despite Solzhenitsyn's literal-mindedness and its resultant literary inadequacies, despite the frequent use of political journalism instead of literary art, Solzhenitsyn has written a profoundly felt, acutely observed, and sharply rendered novel in the grand style. *The First Circle* succeeds in bringing together a wide range of characters in a polyphonic arrangement of their personalities and fates. By stripping Soviet social and human realities of their official Potemkin façades, the novel shows to the Russian people and others just what Soviet society has lost in giving up "socialism with a human face." Thereby Solzhenitsyn has sought to recover some of the traditional Russian artistic responsibility for the great problems of his time and place, some obligation for the regeneration of Soviet life and literature.

4 ⸶ Cancer Ward: ⸶ The Malignant Tumors

After all, man is a complicated being, why should he be explainable by logic? Or for that matter by economics? Or physiology? Yes, I did come to you as a corpse, and I begged you to take me in, and I lay on the floor by the staircase. And therefore you make the logical deduction that I came to you to be saved *at any price!* But I don't want to be saved at any price. There isn't anything in the world for which I'd agree to pay *any* price!

Aleksandr Solzhenitsyn

In his first two novels Solzhenitsyn chose a concentration camp and a prison research institute for metaphors of Soviet society; in his third novel he picked a cancer ward in a hospital as the metaphor, and it goes a step beyond the other two in his delineation of life. Where the *sharashka* and the penal colony are man-made institutions imposed on other men, cancer is a malignancy in the very nature of man, and precisely because Solzhenitsyn was now to focus on the evil in the nature of man, he chose it for his central symbol. In *Cancer Ward*, Solzhenitsyn deals with two major ethical problems: freedom and personal sovereignty;

and evil and disease. Both are portrayed as subsuming all the difficulties of Soviet institutions, but the problems are the primary focus and not the institutions themselves. That may be the reason *Cancer Ward* seemed less threatening to the Soviet authorities at first and may explain how the novel managed to make its way through the obstacle course of the Soviet literary bureaucracy to the point where a considerable section of it was set into type for *Novy mir*, though ultimately it was denied publication.

If *Cancer Ward* is not so specifically political as its predecessor, its title and contents indicate that it views the world, and Soviet society in particular, as a malignant place in which the doctors themselves are sick, in which the physicians not only cannot heal the patients but cannot heal themselves, and in which they guess at solutions and treatments—x-rays, hormones, surgery, chemotherapy—which they hope will be efficacious in curing, but which are all in themselves crippling. It is a view of the nature of man and society which Soviet authorities have always been reluctant to permit to circulate in their domain. Moreover, the novel also had its own important and specific threat to the Soviet authorities, for to a much greater extent than in *Ivan Denisovich* or *The First Circle*, the heirs of Stalin are among its chief targets, and the time in which the novel is set was not the Stalinist past but the post-Stalin period.

As in his other novels, Solzhenitsyn continued to write out of what he had himself personally and painfully experienced, and the events of his life and those of his protagonist in *Cancer Ward* are remarkably coincident. Like the author, Oleg Kostoglotov is a war veteran who has served a term in a concentration camp, where, before being released after Stalin's death, he was operated on for cancer. Subsequently condemned to perpetual exile in Kazakhstan—Solzhenitsyn actually lived at Kok-Terek (Green Poplar); he has Kostoglotov living at Ush-Terek (Three Poplars)—he finds that the cancer has recurred and makes his way, half-dead, to a cancer-treatment hospital in Tashkent, where development of the tumor is arrested by modern medical treatment. In some small ways Solzhenitsyn differentiates Kostoglotov's history and character from his own and from those of the even closer prototype, Gleb Nerzhin. Solzhenitsyn and Nerzhin were both captains in World War II, Kostoglotov a sergeant; they were both born in 1918, Kostoglotov in 1920; they are both mathematicians and university graduates, while his is a land surveyor who was never graduated from a university. But Kostoglotov has the reflective and rebellious character of his creator, the same profound commitments to political and historical justice, to personal freedom and sovereignty.

Cancer Ward is set in the Tashkent hospital, and the action of the novel takes place over a period of approximately four months, from the winter to the spring of 1955, during which time Kostoglotov's cancer and the national cancer of Stalinism are both presumably arrested. Just as Kostoglotov's tumor subsides in virulence and is reduced in size, so too do the tumors of Stalinism begin to be brought under control. Solzhenitsyn deliberately chooses the change from winter to spring as part of the "thaw" which, alternating with freezes, has characterized most of Soviet cultural and political life—and also characterizes the natural seasonal cycle of Russian climate.

From the opening pages, with the introduction of Pavel Nikolayevich Rusanov entering the hospital, Solzhenitsyn juxtaposes biological and social cancer. The epitome of the heirs of Stalin, Rusanov is a petty, overbearing, cowardly, and not especially intelligent Stalinist bureaucrat, a man almost altogether without saving graces. His job as a "personnel specialist"—the euphemism for a member of the KGB—is to search out and denounce "enemies of the regime" and to help fabricate cases against them. The first chapter is called "No Cancer Whatsoever," both because Rusanov denies that he has cancer—a not unusual human refusal to accept serious biological illness—and because the political allegory is meant to indicate that the Rusanovs of the Soviet Union see no serious tumors in the body politic. Even as Rusanov denies that he has cancer, the tumor juts out of his throat "the size of a clenched fist" [1] —the traditional Communist gesture—and the descriptions of the hospital, shabby, dilapidated, overcrowded, and understaffed, and of Rusanov's and his family's behavior begin the revelations of the social and political cancers.

In his conduct at the hospital, Rusanov exemplifies the immorality, materialism, snobbery, status consciousness, coarseness, and arbitrariness of the true heirs of Stalin. He

[1] *Cancer Ward*, trans. Nicholas Bethell and David Burg (Farrar, Straus & Giroux), p. 6.

hates being taken into the clinic like "an ordinary patient, just like anyone else, and superstitiously he is alarmed because the ward he is assigned to is Number 13 (pp. 1–2). Rusanov doesn't want to sit on the same bench in the reception room with the peasants waiting there, especially because some of them are Uzbeks—Rusanov is a Great Russian—and the sight and smell of their poverty offend him to the core. With him are his wife, Kapitolina, and his eldest son, Yuri. His wife, two silver foxes ostentatiously draped over her shoulders, is the model of a *nouvelle arrivée:* she disregards the hospital ordinances, patronizes the employees and other patients, and to the embarrassment of her son tries to bribe the reception nurse to obtain special privileges for her husband.

Once assigned to the cancer ward itself, Rusanov is infuriated at being told by one of his ward mates that he has cancer or he wouldn't be there; and he is also outraged that the doctors do not come to give him immediate attention. He thinks of them in terms of the Stalinist epithet of the 1953 Doctors' Plot, as "assassins in white coats"; when the doctors do arrive the next morning, he blusters and threatens the senior oncologist and head of the radiotherapy ward, Ludmila Dontsova, that he will call his "contacts" in the Ministry of Health and the local Party boss, Ostapenko. Dontsova, however, refuses to be bullied. Instead she gives him an ultimatum: either he decides to accept treatment that very day—he has announced that he will go to a Moscow hospital—or he leaves. Rusanov, crushed, accepts.

Despite that "defeat," Rusanov believes that his position
and past entitle him to certain privileges which Solzhenitsyn's protagonist, Kostoglotov, refuses to extend to him.
In this conflict, sometimes petty but more often profound,
between the former concentration-camp prisoner and exile
in perpetuity and the KGB official and informer, Solzhenitsyn intends more than the mere polarized symbolism of
prisoner and jailer; he is also presenting continuing conflict
between conformist and nonconformist, "liberal" and "dog-
matist," individualist and bureaucrat in the Soviet Union.
Rusanov forever thinks and speaks in *Pravda* clichés, but
Solzhenitsyn has him reveal the realities beneath those
banalities. While reading a *Pravda* announcement that there
are going to be changes in the nation, Rusanov reflects:

> Yes, the economy was advancing by leaps and
> bounds; and this would mean, of course, major
> changes in a number of state and economic organi-
> zations. . . . These reorganizations were always
> rather exciting; they served as a temporary diversion
> from everyday work; the officials would be telephon-
> ing each other, holding meetings and discussing the
> possibilities. And whichever direction the reorganiza-
> tions took . . . no one, including Pavel Nikolaye-
> vich, ever suffered a drop in rank. There were only
> promotions. [p. 17]

Rusanov is a man in whom self-interest and material
concerns are paramount, the cornerstones on which he has
built his life and his career. Both he and his wife started

out as workers in the dough-kneading section (a double entendre?) of a macaroni factory before their faithful work in Komsomol, Party, and KGB brought them to their present "eminence." His KGB career had been launched with his denunciation of his friend and neighbor, Rodichev, with whom the Rusanovs had shared a factory-awarded common apartment. Quarters had been too cramped for the growing Rusanov family, so Rusanov had denounced Rodichev as a counterrevolutionary and saboteur in order to acquire the entire flat for himself. Rodichev's wife was pregnant, and since the law prevented them from throwing her into the street after Rodichev was imprisoned on Rusanov's denunciation, the Rusanovs had let her remain in the flat until she gave birth, albeit encouraging their four-year-daughter, Alla, to spit in her saucepans in their common kitchen.

As time went on, Rusanov's denunciations grew bolder and more open. He was even able to summon up enough courage to confront those he denounced, although usually this was not necessary; in any event, he was afraid of such confrontations, because he particularly feared being physically assaulted by one of those whom he had denounced. It was the peak time of his life.

In that excellent and honorable time, the years 1937 and 1938, the social atmosphere was noticeably cleansed and it became easier to breathe. The liars and slanderers, those who had been too bold in their criticism, the clever-dick intellectuals, all of them disappeared, shut up or lay low, while the men of principle, the loyal and stable men, Rusanov's friends and Rusanov himself, were able to walk with dignity, their heads held high. [p. 191]

His work, of course, brought rewards from the state. Rusanov was paid well, and soon had his own car, his cottage in the country, his small house in town, and his assured pension. With the years, too, the Rusanovs began to hate any brush with ordinary people. They stopped traveling on buses, trolleys, and public transport of any kind; they switched to taxis, office limousines, and then to their own personal car. On trains, when they had to travel by rail, they no longer sat in the ordinary sections but were assigned their own reserved compartments; on vacation, they had private hotel rooms in resorts where the beaches and the walks and gardens were fenced off from the general public.

The Rusanovs loved the People, their great People. They served the People and were ready to give their lives for the People.

But as the years went by they found themselves less and less able to tolerate actual human beings, those obstinate creatures who were always resistant, refusing to do what they were told and, besides, demanding something for themselves. [p. 196]

Combined with the passion for possessions and power, the distaste for the masses, are the status-seeking and snobbery of a new and insecure class. Rusanov is anxious about his son, Yuri, for example, because the young man is too "soft-hearted," and he worries that the boy "might be led up the garden path by some ordinary weaver girl from the textile factory. . . . It was such an easy step to take, rashly signing your name in the marriage register, and it would ruin not only the young man's life, but his family's too' (pp. 182–183). Rusanov recalls the dilemma of a KGB colleague whose daughter was involved with a country boy from a kolkhoz:

> Just imagine the Shendyapins' flat, their furniture and the influential people they had as guests, and suddenly there's this old woman in a white headscarf sitting at their table, their daughter's mother-in-law, and she didn't even have a passport. Whatever next? Thank goodness they'd managed to discredit the fiancé politically and save their daughter.[2]

But conditions in the Soviet Union in 1955 are beginning to change, and Rusanov is bewildered and frightened. "The finest civic actions of earlier days [during the Great Purges] were now shameful. Would he now have to fear for his own skin?" (p. 191). Earlier, he had named his second son Lavrenti, after the former Minister of State Security, Beria, but now he regrets the action, because "for over a year now you had to be very careful about

[2] P. 183. Kolkhoz members are not permitted to travel, or to leave their place of employment without permission. They are not therefore entitled to carry the internal passports other Soviet citizens are required to carry.

saying the words 'Lavrenti Pavlovich' aloud" (p. 183).
On this he reflects:

> All right, let's suppose Beria *was* a double-dealer, a
> bourgeois nationalist and a seeker after power. Very
> well, put him on trial and shoot him behind closed
> doors, but why tell the ordinary people anything
> about it? Why shake their faith? Why create doubt
> in their minds? When it was all over, one might
> perhaps send out a confidential circular down to a
> certain level to explain the details but as for the news-
> papers, wouldn't it be better to say he died of a
> heart attack and bury him with full honors? [p. 184]

When Rusanov's wife comes to visit him, she informs him
that the new political changes now threaten them personally, because Rodichev, the man he denounced to get
the apartment, has been released from camp and rehabilitated. Rusanov is terrified at the prospect of what
will happen when "they all start coming back"; self-pity-
ingly (and with Solzhenitsyn's stinging irony), he bursts
out: "What *right* have they to let these people out now?
Have they no pity? How dare they cause such traumas?"
(p. 186).

Coming from Moscow to visit him, his daughter Aviette
(Alla) brings him even more upsetting news—that a massive review of legal proceedings has been launched in the
capital. Her self-serving comments further illuminate the
mentality both of the younger and the older heirs of
Stalin, all of whom want most to save their skins, to retain

their power and privilege, to circumvent punishment and prevent revenge, to avoid ugly confrontations with those whom they have condemned and denounced.

> The pendulum's swung right the other way. As if the wheel of history can ever be turned back! . . . All right, granted it was a long time ago they convicted those people, rightly or wrongly, and sent them far away into exile—but why bring them back now? Why transplant them back to their former lives? It's a painful, agonizing process. Above all it's cruel to the exiles themselves. Some of them are dead— why disturb their ghosts? Why raise groundless hopes among their relatives and perhaps a desire for revenge? Again, what does rehabilitated actually mean? It can't mean the man was completely innocent! He must have done *something*, however trivial. [p. 281]

Rusanov is not only threatened by the revisions of "violations of socialist legality," but by de-Stalinization. On March 5, 1955, lying in bed in the cancer ward, Rusanov carefully peruses *Pravda* to see what attention will be paid to the second anniversary of Stalin's death, whether the entire paper will have a black mourning border, a full-page portrait of the dictator, a banner headline. Only a few months previous, in December 1954, the old fanfare had accompanied the celebrations of Stalin's seventy-fifth birthday, but now there is only a small feature article tucked away obscurely and without any accompanying picture, written by a member of the Academy of Sciences instead of a leading political leader. Rusanov is almost completely disheartened.

> It wasn't the danger, no, it wasn't the danger that now threatened those who were left after his death. . . . It was this ingratitude that wounded Rusanov most of all, as though his own great services, his own irreproachable record were what they were spitting on and trampling underfoot. . . . If the Most Beloved, the Most Wise, the One whom all your superiors and superiors' superiors obeyed, could be overturned and hushed up within twenty-four months—then what remained? What could one rely on? *How could a man recover his health in such circumstances?* [p. 314—italics added]

This fear and disenchantment, this trembling and loss of faith, are an accurate picture of the disarray caused in the Soviet bureaucracy by de-Stalinization and its legal and personal consequences.

Rusanov's family is afflicted not only by the "heirs of Stalin" problem but also by the problem of "fathers and sons." Yuri, Rusanov's eldest son, is a lawyer about to go off on his first assignment when his father enters the cancer ward; Rusanov is constrained to advise him to cultivate hardness and inhumanity: "Be sure to set the right tone from the start. And don't be too soft, mind. Your softness could be your downfall. Always remember you're not Yuri Rusanov, you're not a private individual. You're a representative of the law, do you understand?" (p. 7).

Troubled by his son's compassion, Rusanov worries that the young man will bungle his job, making a fool both of himself and his family—and he is worried not only about opprobrium but also about repercussions more serious and dangerous.

Rusanov vastly prefers his daughter Alla, who wants to be a journalist and writer, and who is cut on the same bias as her parents. Like her father, she can sniff the wind accurately, and from her observations of the Moscow scene she brings to her father a clear definition of the "middle course" the Khrushchev regime is following in de-Stalinization: "Though they talk about the 'cult of personality,' in the same breath they speak of 'the great successor.' So one mustn't go too far in either direction" (p. 283). In short, if Stalin "made errors" that culminated in the cult of personality, he also remained the great continuer of Lenin, so his flaws were balanced by his virtues, his crimes by his accomplishments.

Rusanov is eager for his son and daughter to understand him and his life. "It's very important for young people to understand us," he remarks, "and not condemn" (p. 282). But when son Yuri returns to visit his father after his first official trip, Rusanov is altogether unable to understand the young man. "Clearly, his son had not returned from his assignment with a clear conscience," Solzhenitsyn observes. "He kept averting his gaze instead of looking his father in the eye" (p. 401). Yuri horrifies his father by telling him what he has done as part of the republic's legal inspection team in a remote town. He has suspended the execution of a five-year sentence imposed on a truck driver who, his machine stuck in a snowstorm in ten-below-zero weather and himself in danger of freezing to death, had left his truck to find warmth. When he returned, a case of macaroni was missing, and for that he was sentenced to five years. Rusanov berates his son for naïveté and gullibility, maintaining that like a sentry in wartime, the truck driver should have died at his post. "Yuri was making a mess of his job, ruining himself and casting a shadow over his father's reputation" (p. 403).

An opponent of, and contrast to, the KGB bureaucrat with wife, children, possessions, and status is the novel's protagonist, Oleg Kostoglotov, a World War II combat veteran and former prisoner of the concentration camps, who is still condemned to perpetual exile—a loner without wife or children and with only those few possessions he can carry on his back. Intelligent, sensitive, self-taught but educated, the thirty-four-year-old Kostoglotov is the archdisciple of personal freedom and individual sovereignty. Where Rusanov is comfortable only as part of the great bureaucratic machine, Kostoglotov resists all bureaucracies—army, police, medical—seeking only to exercise and assert his independence. As Kostoglotov puts it to the cancer-ward doctor, Vera Gangart, while trying to explain why he did not become an officer during the war: "I was too devoted to democracy. I tried to spread democracy in the army, that is, I answered my superiors back" (p. 222). Rusanov's opinions are the clichés of a Stalinist

KGB bureaucrat; Kostoglotov is a prickly autodidact not prepared to accept anyone else's word for anything without questioning and investigating on his own. When Rusanov proclaims, "There are questions on which a definite opinion has been established, and they are no longer open to discussion" (p. 138), Kostoglotov explodes. "No one on this earth ever says anything 'once and for all.' If they did, life would come to a stop and succeeding generations would have nothing to say" (p.139). Rusanov, then, is closed to new concepts, comfortable only with "received ideas," while Kostoglotov is eager to learn and open to new and unorthodox notions. Perhaps most important in differentiating the two men are Rusanov's passion for power, possessions, and privilege and Kostoglotov's obsession with justice, equality, and freedom.

Kostoglotov's arrival at the hospital is deliberately contrived to be a dramatic contrast to Rusanov's. Rusanov walks in accompanied by wife and son, with his own personal pajamas and cache of food, and is treated with gingerly respect and care. Kostoglotov arrives at night, half-dead, and stretches out on the floor of the admission ward to sleep, because there is nowhere for him to be put—no bed, no bench. When rebuked for such "unseemly" behavior, he replies: "This is my country. Why should I be ashamed?" (p. 62).

Kostoglotov has a cancer of the stomach and is dying, but x-ray treatments by Dontsova and Gangart—he has an extraordinary resistance to the x-rays which is of great help—soon give him back his taste for life. With freedom from pain, his sexual desire also returns. Despite such "success," Kostoglotov rebels against treatment and the whole framework of hospital medicine, because they deprive him of his freedom. Fearful of the destructive consequences of the x-rays, he tries to explain to the head radiologist, Dontsova, why he is averse to continuing the treatment:

> I simply wanted to remind you of my right to dispose of my own life. A man can dispose of his own life, can't he? You agree I have that right? . . .
> . . . You start from a completely false position. No sooner does a patient come to you than you begin to do all his thinking for him. After that, the thinking's done by your standing orders, your five-minute conferences, your program, your plan and the honor of your medical department. And once again I become a grain of sand, just as I was in the camp. Once again nothing *depends* on me. [p. 76]

In telling Dontsova about his first bout with cancer, he tries to explain the conditions of the concentration camp to her and finds that she is unable to understand that doctors are taken on transports from one camp to another in the midst of an operation, leaving patients without medical care, and do not keep proper records of case histories; as a result, he cannot get her a histological analysis of his first tumor. Dontsova does not believe any of this, and Kostoglotov reflects that she "was his compatriot, his contemporary and well-wisher. They were talking in their own language, common to them both, and still he couldn't explain the simplest thing to her" (p. 72). Dontsova berates him because he has complained of the medical neglect in the camps and is now protesting against her treatment; she remarks that he is not being "logical," and Kostoglotov replies:

> Obviously there's no logic. . . . After all, man is a complicated being, why should he be explainable by logic? Or for that matter by economics? Or physiology? Yes, I did come to you as a corpse, and I begged you to take me in, and I lay on the floor by the staircase. And therefore you make the logical deduction that I came to you to be saved *at any price!* But I don't want to be saved at any price! There isn't anything in the world for which I'd agree to pay *any* price! [p. 77]

One price Kostoglotov is unwilling to pay is the loss of his personal sovereignty. "Why do you assume you have the right to decide for someone else?" he asks Dontsova. "Don't you agree it's a terrifying right, one that rarely leads to good? . . . No one's entitled to it, not even doctors" (p. 79).

Solzhenitsyn is talking not only of medicine here, but of politics, of the perennial question of ends and means, insisting that the individual has the right to refuse the means even if he is assured that the end will be good for him. In medicine, he comments, every decade or so doctors discover that what they were doing earlier was primitive, barbarous, ineffective, dangerous, or all of these together. For years, for example, radiologists had x-rayed patients with impunity, until in time they saw results cropping up which later led them to understand radiation sickness. What Kostoglotov is in search of is a "natural" way to cure his illness, not x-rays or injections or transfusions. In fact, he has been treating himself with two "natural" medicines, one a mandrake root from Issyk Kul and the other a birchbark tea called *chaga*, and he is not altogether sure that they did not contribute to his recovery. Outraged by such presumption and "superstition," Dontsova remains "unshakably convinced that any damage to the body was justified if it saved life" (p. 88). When Dr. Gangart discovers Kostoglotov with some of the Issyk Kul root medicine, she forces him to pour it out; she declares, "I believe in systematic science, practically tested" (p. 231).

Solzhenitsyn seems also to be talking about the categorical wisdom of "scientific socialism," comparing medical tyranny and political tyranny, commenting that both diagnose, kill, and cure with very imperfect knowledge of the results they set out to achieve. When the physicians use x-ray therapy, they destroy healthy as well as cancerous tissue; when they use hormone therapy, they destroy sexuality and fertility; when they employ surgery, they lop off limbs and organs which cannot be replaced: "It was a universal law: everyone who *acts* breeds both good and evil. With some it's more good, with others more evil" (p. 90). The allegorical identification of cancer ward and Soviet state is not perfectly clear. Solzhenitsyn seems to be implying that the means employed by the Soviet state in curing the Russian body politic of the illnesses of tsarism were unnatural—did not take into consideration the nature of man—and therefore failed. When Rusanov explains selfish behavior in terms of "survivals of bourgeois mentality," Kostoglotov denies such nonsensical clichés, maintaining, "It's human greed . . . not bourgeois mentality. There were greedy people *before* the bourgeoisie and there'll be greedy people *after* the bourgeoisie" (p. 409); he goes on to denounce Rusanov for his use of class origins, calling it racism, not Marxism. Rusanov counters by accusing him of ideological sabotage, and Kostoglotov in a rage roars: "Go and —— yourself, you and your ideological sabotage! A fine habit you've developed, you mother- . . . . Every time someone disagrees with you, you call it ideological sabotage!" (p. 410).

But the equation of the decent, dedicated physician Dontsova, who because of her work at the oncology clinic gets cancer, with the head of the state, Stalin, who was eaten away by megalomania and paranoia, who was neither benevolent nor curative, is hard to believe. So is the equation of doctor with commissar, scientific medicine with "scientific socialism." Solzhenitsyn, however, may be suggesting that in spite of the evil means employed by Stalin, in spite of his killing off "good tissue"—decent people and institutions—the dictator did cure some of the ills of tsarism by creating the industrial and military power of contemporary Russia.

If one carries the equation still further, it becomes even

more baffling. When Dontsova is finally moved to discover whether or not she herself has cancer, she goes to see her former teacher, Dr. Dormidont Oreshchenkov, a man seventy-five years old who has treated disease for half a century. An early revolutionary whose father was an Orthodox priest and who was himself a medical officer and hero in the tsarist army during World War I, Orshchenkov has been consistently persecuted by the Soviet regime because of his "stubborn insistence on his right to maintain a private medical practice" (p. 420). He is an old-fashioned all-around doctor, who was trained in all the branches of medicine before he specialized in cancer treatment and diagnosis; and he believes in free choice of physicians, in family doctors, not specialists, in patients paying their own way, in doctors depending on the confidence and good will of their patients. He also wants physicians to know and understand the whole patient, to treat the whole patient, not merely the symptom, and to answer all the patient's questions as well. He is a physician of the old school—you might say the best kind of free-enterprise doctor—who prizes the individual, freedom, equality, and personal responsibility. Dontsova, though she is herself a highly skilled physician, does not want to participate either in the diagnosis or treatment of her illness; she has always believed that the patient has no right to know. In short, she wishes to surrender her sovereignty to Oreshchenkov —precisely what Kostoglotov has been unwilling to do for her or for Gangart. Solzhenitsyn may be suggesting that the physician must go back to older, more tried and true ways of dealing with human and social illness if he is to heal himself. He may even be suggesting a return to the Leninist NEP methods. Moreover, the self-cure use of folk medicines which Solzhenitsyn seems drawn to and which his protagonist Kostoglotov defends may be more than superstition; it may be a declaration that "scientific medicine" and "scientific socialism" are no more effective than the Issyk Kul root derivative or the birchbark *chaga*, that perhaps the people's wisdom about what is effective for their physical ailments is as good as the physician's, and that perhaps the same is true of their social and political ailments and their leaders' judgments.

Solzhenitsyn suggests a connection between cancer and the individual, between social cancer and the behavior of the state. He adds a psychosomatic dimension to the problem by implying that there is an inextricable connection between violation of conscience and law, betrayal, guilt, sin, remorse, and anxiety and the development of both individual and social cancers. Rusanov, the informer, for instance, gets cancer of the throat. Vadim, the young geologist who is pro-Stalin because the dictator "exalted science, exalted scientists and freed them from petty thoughts of salary or accommodations" (p. 315), relies only on science, lacks humanity, and is stricken with melanoblastoma, the most virulent of cancers, in one of his legs and creeping up toward his groin. (An additional irony is that he is obsessed with finding a way to discover ores by following radioactive waters, and what he needs to cure him, or more accurately, to arrest the tumor's spread, is colloidal gold, which he has great difficulty in procuring.) Not only will he very likely have his leg amputated, but he has only a short time to live. Dyomka, the young student, who is both an idealist and a humanist, who loves truth and literature but does not know very much about science or mathematics, also has cancer of the leg—sarcoma in his case, less lethal—but he too must have his leg amputated. Solzhenitsyn seems to be saying that science without the humanities is death; the humanities without science, crippling, Asya, the young girl patient with whom Dyomka falls in love, is completely devoted to the physical life, to dancing, athletics, and sex; she is afflicted with cancer of the breast and must endure having a breast removed. Yefrem Podduyev, the former concentration-camp guard, whose quick tongue has been ever ready, with women and with others—"With it he piled filth on everything most dear and holy" (p. 97)—has cancer of the tongue.

Aleksei Shulubin, the Old Bolshevik, has cancer of the rectum and will have to have surgery and a colostomy bag to survive. Shulubin confesses to Kostoglotov that such a thing will be especially humiliating; people will not even want to be near him if he survives the surgery, because the stench will offend them. Shulubin's stench is not only a medical kind but a moral kind: he has been servile and silent for twenty-five years for his wife's sake, for his children's sake, and then for his own sake—for the sake of "my own sinful body. But my wife died. And my body is a bag full of manure. . . . And my children have grown up so callous it's beyond comprehension" (p. 441). Shulubin was a Bolshevik in 1917, fought against the Mensheviks and Social Revolutionaries in Tambov and then in the Civil War, but he claims he was a "little man" who couldn't bring himself to speak out against the horrors. Why, he asks, didn't such "great people" as Krupskaya, Lenin's widow, or Ordzhonikidze, the Party leader and Stalin's friend, speak up? Shulubin asserts that it was even worse to be a coward and hypocrite, as he was, than to be a prisoner and outcast as Kostoglotov was.

> You haven't had to do much lying. . . . At least you haven't had to stoop so low. . . . You people were arrested, but we were herded into meetings to "expose" you. They executed people like you, but they made us stand up and applaud the verdicts as they were announced. And not just applaud, they made us demand the firing squad, *demand* it! . . . Who ever came out in your defense? Who ever objected? Where are they now? I knew one—Dima Olitsky— he abstained. He wasn't opposed, good heavens no! He *abstained* on the vote to shoot the Industrial Party members. "Explain!" they shouted. "Explain!" He stood up, his throat was dry as a bone. "I believe," he said, "that in the twelfth year of the Revolution we should be able to find alternative methods of repression. . . ." Aaah, the scoundrel! Accomplice! Enemy agent! The next morning he got a summons

to the G.P.U., and there he stayed for the rest of his
life. [pp. 436–437]

Shulubin is here defending and extending Ilya Ehrenburg's argument about the "conspiracy of silence" during
the Stalinist era, for which Ehrenburg had been so sharply
attacked by Galina Serebryakova and others.[3] Shulubin
states categorically that people *did* know about the perse-
cutions; they did not believe the charges leveled against
those who were condemned.

> Suddenly all the professors and all the engineers turn
> out to be wreckers, and he believes it! The best
> Civil-War divisional commanders turn out to be
> German and Japanese spies, and he believes it! The
> whole of Lenin's old guard are shown up as vile rene-
> gades, and he believes it! His own friends and ac-
> quaintances are unmasked as enemies of the people,
> and he believes it! Millions of Russian soldiers turn
> out to have betrayed their country, and he believes it
> all! Whole nations, old men and babies, are mown
> down, and he believes it! Then what sort of man is
> he, may I ask? He's a fool. But can there really be
> a whole nation of fools? No, you'll have to forgive
> me. The people are intelligent enough, it's simply
> that they wanted to live. There's a law big nations
> have—to endure and so to survive. When each of us
> dies and History stands over his grave and asks "What

[3] See Priscilla Johnson, *Khrushchev and the Arts* (Cambridge:
M.I.T. Press, 1965), pp. 11–30 *passim*.

was he?" there'll only be one possible answer, Pushkin's:

> In our vile times
> . . . Man was, whatever his element,
> Either tyrant or traitor or prisoner! [p. 438]

Shulubin's career is a paradigm of the life of the driven
scientific intellectual during three decades of Soviet life.
A graduate of the most prestigious agricultural school in
the Soviet Union, the Timiryazev Academy, he was gradually driven by the regime's coercion from his position as a
university lecturer in Moscow, and then step by step to
the very lowest position, because of the need to hide and
save himself.

> We were supposed to confess our "mistakes"? I
> confessed them! We were supposed to renounce
> them? I renounced them! A certain percentage man-
> aged to survive, didn't they? Well, I was part of
> that percentage. I withdrew into the study of pure
> biology. I found myself a quiet haven. But then the
> purge started there as well, and what a purge! The
> professional chairs in the biological department got
> a thorough sweeping with the broom. We were sup-
> posed to give up lecturing? Very well, I gave up
> lecturing. I withdrew even further, became an assis-
> tant. I agreed to become a little man! . . .
> They were destroying textbooks written by great

scientists, they were changing the curricula. Very well, I agreed to that too; we would use the new books for teaching! They suggested we reshape anatomy, microbiology and neuropathology to fit in with the doctrines of an ignorant agronomist and an expert in horticulture. Bravo! I agreed! I voted in favor! "No, that's not enough. Will you please give up your assistantship as well?" "All right, I'm not arguing. I'll work on methods of biology teaching in schools." But no, the sacrifice wasn't accepted. I was sacked from that job as well. "Very well, I agree, I'll be a librarian, a librarian in remote Kokand." I retreated a long, long way! Still, I was alive, and my children were university graduates. But then librarians receive secret instructions from the authorities: for the destruction of books by this or that author. Well, this was nothing new for us. Had I not declared a quarter of a century earlier from my chair of dialectical materialism that the relativity theory was counterrevolutionary obscurantism? So I draw up a document, my Party secretary and special-branch representative signs it, and we stuff the books into the stove. Into the stove with all your genetics, leftist aesthetics, ethics, cybernetics, arithmetic. [pp. 441–442]

Is it any wonder that Sulubin, a man who has in the most vulgar but literal sense eaten so much shit, is now to stink of it, to have difficulty in digesting it physically, and will, if he survives his colostomy, alienate the company of men with his stench?

Solzhenitsyn explains what he has been driving at in a scene in which Kostoglotov reads from a textbook on pathological anatomy to the other patients in the cancer ward. "It says here that the link between the development of tumors and the central nervous system has so far been very little studied. And this link is an amazing thing! . . . 'It happens rarely, but there are cases of self-induced healing.' " To this, Yefrem Podduyev, the former KGB man with cancer of the tongue, responds, "I suppose for that you need to have . . . a clear conscience" (p. 136). Kostoglotov then makes the point that attitudes of mind frequently determine physiological chemical balance and resistance to disease, and that perhaps "in a hundred years' time they [may] discover that our organism excretes some kind of cesium salt when our conscience is clear, but not when it's burdened, and that it depends on this cesium salt whether the cells grow into a tumor or whether the tumor resolves" (p. 138). Man's frame of mind, man's conscience, may in the long, and even in the short run, determine his physical health and his freedom from malignancy. The same may be true for a nation. As Solzhenitsyn writes about Rusanov and his cancer:

> His fate lay there, between his chin and his collarbone.
> There justice was being done.
> And in answer to this justice he could summon no influential friend, no past services, no defense. [p. 199]

Solzhenitsyn deals more extensively with love and sex in *Cancer Ward* than in the other novels, and does so in a curiously ambiguous fashion. Yet the very ambiguity is intriguing, for it seems likely that the love-sex relationships explored in the novel would have been more explicit had he felt freer to write as he pleased and not been oppressed by the puritanism of contemporary Soviet writing. In spite of the occasional epithet, four-letter word, and mother oath—anathema to such puritanical dogmatists as *Oktyabr* editor Vsevolod Kochetov—Solzhenitsyn's writing about sex and love is tender and moving, and the intensified sexuality of the book is quite justified by the hospital context, where sex and love become an affirmation of the desire to recover and to live.

Three important love affairs, two of them involving Kostoglotov, are the main focus here, and in all three Solzhenitsyn seems bent on dealing with sexual matters in much the same psychological-physiological way that he deals with cancer. The love affair between the young Dyomka and Asya is a case in point. Asya is a "modern" girl whose chief interests are physical: football, dancing, rock-and-roll music. Assured, self-confident, without doubts or anxieties, she counsels Dyomka not to permit his cancerous leg to be amputated. "Life is made for happiness," Asya reminds him. "It's better to die than live without a leg. What sort of life is it for a cripple . . . ?" (p. 131). Though Dyomka comes from a home where sex was made disgusting to him because his mother was a whore, his affection for Asya makes sex seem innocent and unsullied for the first time. Dyomka is a virgin, but

161

Asya has already had considerable sexual experience—
since the ninth grade in school. "Why wait?" she asks.
"It's the atomic age!" (p. 134). Solzhenitsyn's tone clearly
indicates disapproval of such casual attitudes toward sex,
a disapproval he makes all the more explicit in recounting
Yefrem Podduyev's foot-loose sexual encounters. When
Asya discovers that she has cancer of the breast and must
have the breast removed, Solzhenitsyn writes a scene suggesting that in the end emotion and spirit are what count
in the relations between the sexes, not the body, but the
argument is one to which he is only partially committed—
as Kostoglotov's final resolution of his love affairs subsequently makes plain.

Asya is shattered by the doctors' diagnosis calling for
the amputation of her right breast and goes to Dyomka
for solace. Weeping, feeling that she has nothing left to
live for, that no one in the world will ever want her again,
she is disconsolate. Dyomka comforts her, or tries to, by
remarking that people marry because they have interests
in common, similar characters; Asya chastens him tartly:
"What sort of fool loves a girl for a character? Who
wants a girl with one breast? Who wants a girl like that?
When she's seventeen!" (p. 398). Fumblingly, feelingly
Dyomka tells her that he will always be happy to marry
her, and suddenly dry-eyed, Asya opens her dressing
gown and proffers her doomed right breast, declaring that
he will be the last one to see it and kiss it.

> "Kiss it! Kiss it!" she demanded. She stood there
> waiting.

And breathing in the warmth her body was offering him, he nuzzled it with his lips like a suckling pig, gratefully, admiringly. Nothing more beautiful than this gentle curve could ever be painted or sculptured. Its beauty flooded him. Hurriedly his lips took in its even, shapely contour.

"You'll remember? . . . You'll remember, won't you? You'll remember it was there, and what it was like?" Asya's tears kept dropping onto his close-cropped head.

When she did not take it away, he returned to its rosy glow again and again, softly kissing the breast. He did what her future child would never be able to do. No one came in, and so he kissed and kissed the marvel hanging over him.

Today it was a marvel. Tomorrow it would be in the trash bin. [p. 399]

Kostoglotov's most painful decision in the cancer ward is not political but sexual: he must choose between saving his life and retaining his virility; between accepting and continuing the course of injections of female hormones prescribed to arrest the tumors and refusing those injections and so risking the recurrence of the cancer and perhaps the loss of his life. His two love affairs exemplify the choices: one, with the twenty-two-year-old nurse Zoya is primarily physical; the second, with a woman closer to his own age, Dr. Vera Gangart, primarily spiritual. With the beginning of his recovery, Kostoglotov starts to feel the return of his sexual desire and potency—and also of his dreams. Knowing that he has returned from the border of death, he finds simple things charged with intense and unexpected pleasure and emotion: women's legs, breasts, lips, clothing, conversation. His desires are made more poignant and are heightened by the long deprivation he has suffered during the years of the war, camp, and exile. There is a delicate scene in which Kostoglotov persuades Zoya to take off her white coat so that he can see her dress beneath. She shows it to him, spinning around like a professional model, and tells him that her name, Zoya, means "life." (Solzhenitsyn also gives Vera a symbolic name—meaning "faith" in Russian—and her nickname, Vega, is the name of the brilliant star of the first magnitude in the constellation Lyra, the fourth brightest star in the heavens and part of the northern constellation which represents the lyre of Orpheus.) Symbolically, their first kiss takes place next to the oxygen tanks where Zoya has gone to get oxygen for a dying patient. Kostoglotov asks her to marry him, to come to Ush-Terek with him to share his exile. Zoya is touched; perhaps this will provide the serious and stable relationship she has longed for instead of another casual sexual affair. It is then she tells Kostoglotov what the hormone injections will do, that they will leave him with his sexual desires but without the capacity to fulfill them. Stunned and horrified, Kostoglotov persuades her to enter into a conspiracy with him *not* to give him the hormone injections.

Kostoglotov's relationship with Vera Gangart proceeds on quite another plane. Vera is the admitting doctor who saw him dying on the floor when he first came to the hospital, and found a bench for him to sleep on. She also caught him dosing himself with the extract of the root from Issyk Kul and forced him to pour it out beneath a flagstone in the walk outside the ward. She insists that he continue both the x-ray and hormone treatment; she even overrides his objections to blood transfusions. Zoya then is conspiring to save his body because that is what he wants —and also what she wants—but Vega insists on saving his life, even if the cure will emasculate him. (During the blood transfusions, Kostoglotov, symbolically, is given a woman's blood.) Solzhenitsyn is trying to epitomize two different kinds of marriage: one based on friendship and common interests, the other on physical passion. In a painful scene during which Vega is transfusing blood into Kostoglotov, he speaks as much to himself as to her, saying, "First my own life was taken from me [by imprisonment], and now I am being deprived even of the right . . . to perpetuate myself. I'll be the worst sort of cripple! What use will I be to anyone? An object of men's pity— or charity?" (p. 337)—a male echo of Asya's lament for her breast. Vega and Kostoglotov discuss a book both read in their youth which expressed the "heartless certainty that psychology is of secondary importance in marriage" (p. 339). Both of them disagree with the author and maintain that the true basis of marriage is the meeting of minds and character. Since the death of her fiancé in the war, Vega has been disappointed in men; now, after fourteen years, she finds a man who can transcend the merely sexual in his relations with women, and she is deeply moved. "She was developing her theory about men and women. Hemingway's supermen were creatures who had not yet raised themselves to human level. . . . This wasn't at all what a woman needed from a man. She needed attention and tenderness and a sense of security . . . a feeling that he was her shield and her shelter" (p. 346). Even at the price of his virility, a loss which because of her growing affection for him may affect her profoundly, Vera refuses to surrender Kostoglotov to the tumor: she will not permit him to abandon the hormone treatment of his seminoma.

Solzhenitsyn portrays one idyllic marriage based on mutual interests and affection, that of the old physician Nikolai Kadmin and his wife Elena, both sentenced to ten years and perpetual exile with Kostoglotov at Ush-Terek. The couple had earned their sentences by sheltering a deserter for two nights during the war, a deserter who shortly after the war was pardoned while they continued their imprisonment and exile. The Kadmins, now past the age of great physical passion, are deeply attached to each other and happy with their simple pleasures: music, gardening, bookbinding, their two dogs; and Solzhenitsyn comments, "It is not our level of prosperity that makes for happiness but the kinship of heart to heart and the way we look at the world" (p. 270).

A chance comment overheard makes Vera aware that Kostoglotov has been flirting with Zoya; hurt and disappointed, she withdraws immediately into the formality

of the doctor-patient relationship with him, "reminded
. . . of the law that men have no need for women of
their own age, they need women who are younger. She
shouldn't forget that her time was past, past" (p. 460).
She says nothing to him, and Kostoglotov cannot understand what has happened.

After importuning Zoya to allow him to make love to
her, Kostoglotov grows frustrated with mere kisses and
caresses, and with the spontaneity gone and the feeling
forced, stops going to see her. On her rounds one day,
Vera notes that Kostoglotov has not been reacting properly to the hormone therapy and questions Zoya about
whether he has been getting the injections regularly. Zoya
lies, says that she *has* been giving him the injections, but
wordlessly, with a flash of her eyes to Kostoglotov, she
cancels their agreement, because the game they had played
was exhausted, and "it would be quite ridiculous to go
outside the limits of the game, take a job in that stupid
Ush-Terek and tie her life to a man who . . . No, it was
out of the question" (p. 375).

Kostoglotov subsequently manages to penetrate Vera's
reserve once more, and they make up. Not long afterward,
his treatment, involving heavy doses of both hormones and
x-rays, is ended. Dontsova, herself about to go off to Moscow to be treated for cancer, discharges him from the
hospital, but in the presence of Vera tells him first: "You
shouldn't hope to achieve the happiness of a family. It'll
be many more years before you can have a normal family
life" (p. 460). Despite the fact that both Vera and Zoya

know this, they both give him their addresses—to Kostoglotov's astonishment—so that he can stay at their apartments while he makes arrangements to return to Ush-Terek.

After a complicated and exhausting first day out of the hospital, Kostoglotov decides to go to Vega's flat. "He could not think of her either with greed or with the fury of passion. His one joy would be to go and lie at her feet like a dog, like a miserable beaten cur, to lie on the floor and breathe on her feet like a cur. That would be a happiness greater than anything he could imagine" (p. 512). He arrives at her house holding two bunches of violets tremulously in his hands, but she is out and, feeling awkward and ridiculous waiting for her, he leaves. He finds himself on a crowded trolley car, jammed against a lovely young girl. "The greatest passion in the world could not have joined them as intimately as that crowd" (p. 524). Her young body arouses his sexual desire, but only as a "blissful torture"—his body makes no physical response. "They had warned him, hadn't they? The libido remains, the libido but nothing else." The knowledge is borne in on him that now, if he goes back to Vega, it will be both torment and deceit.

It would mean his demanding more from her than he could ask from himself.

They had come to a high-minded agreement that spiritual communion was more valuable than anything else; yet, having built this tall bridge by hand together, he saw now that his own hands were weakening. He was on his way to her to persuade her boldly of one thing while thinking agonizingly of something else. [p. 525]

Instead Kostoglotov decides to give up Vega and goes to the railway station for tickets to Ush-Terek.

From the station he writes to Zoya and Vera. He thanks Zoya honestly "for allowing my lips to get a a taste of genuine life. Without those few evenings I should have felt absolutely, yes absolutely, robbed"; and he wishes her a happy marriage in the future (p. 531). To Vega he writes a long, painful letter, saying that if they lived together, something false and forced would begin: ". . . You will come to bless this day, the day you did not commit yourself to share my life. . . . You slaughtered the first half of your life like a lamb. Please spare the second half!" He confesses that "even when we were having the most intellectual conversations and I honestly thought and believed everything I said, I still wanted all the time, *all the time*, to pick you up and kiss you on the lips" (p. 532). However high-minded and idealistic his talk and intentions, then, Kostoglotov's sexuality always urgently intruded itself, so he knows that he cannot content himself, or satisfy her, with a marriage deprived of physical passion. If Solzhenitsyn portrays Kostoglotov's failure to sustain a personal relationship of great intimacy on quite the high-minded and idealistic level Kostoglotov had hoped for, he also shows Kostoglotov as sufficiently high-minded and idealistic to surrender

Vega, primarily because of the anguish and frustration such a "barren" relationship would cause her.

Solzhenitsyn calls for the same kind of idealism in social relations that he calls for in personal relations, though here too he remains uncertain that ordinary human beings can sustain relations on such a level or even achieve them. He has Shulubin tell Kostoglotov: "Don't ever blame socialism for the sufferings and the cruel years you've lived through. However you think about it, history has rejected capitalism once and for all!" (p. 444). Shulubin believes that "scientific socialism," Christian socialism, and even democratic socialism will not do: what is necessary is an "ethical socialism" based, not on materialism or hatred, but on love. Only such a socialism can save. "We have to show the world a society in which all relationships, fundamental principles and laws flow directly from ethics, and from them *alone*. Ethical demands must determine all considerations" (p. 446). Solzhenitsyn carefully points to the Russian roots of such an ethical socialism; they are to be found in the works of the novelist Leo Tolstoy, the religious philosopher Vladimir Soloviev, the populist socialist Nikolai Mikhailovsky, and the great biologist and social thinker Prince Peter Kropotkin. From these roots one must make a tree flower from which people will pluck the fruits of affection. Not happiness, affection. "Happiness is a mirage," Shulubin tells Kostoglotov. "One should never direct people toward happiness. . . . One should direct them toward mutual affection. A beast gnawing at its prey can be happy too, but only human beings can feel affection for each other, and this is the highest achievement they can aspire to." What is true of personal relations is also true of social and political relations.

As for the so-called "happiness of future generations," it's even more of a mirage. Who knows anything about it? Who has spoken with these future generations? Who knows what idols they will worship? Ideas of what happiness is have changed too much through the ages. No one should have the effrontery to try to plan it in advance. When we have enough loaves of white bread to crush them under our heels, when we have enough milk to choke us, we still won't be in the least happy. But if we share things we don't have enough of, we can be happy today! If we care only about "happiness" and about reproducing our species, we shall merely crowd the earth senselessly and create a terrifying society. [p. 447]

Neither material well-being nor sexual gratification is what men require; neither consumer goods nor family life will fulfill them and create a decent, humane society. Only mutual affection and sharing—by implication, a variety of Kropotkin's mutual aid—can make decent men and a decent society.

Solzhenitsyn attempts to exemplify this wisdom in the final chapters of the novel, appropriately entitled, "The First Day of Creation . . ." and ". . . the Last Day," which cover the day Kostoglotov leaves the hospital. As

Kostoglotov walks through the hospital gates, it is spring, and he thinks, "It's just like leaving prison" (p. 489). He goes to town to see a flowering apricot tree and the zoo, which he promised to do for Dyomka. Everything seems new and fresh to his eye and spirit. He has tea at a tea-house, but it is disappointing green tea. Then he sees the "pink miracle" of the flowering apricot in a courtyard, and his spirit soars. He passes a restaurant selling *shashlik*, about which he has heard much in prison. He wants very much to eat some of this meat he has never tasted, but the price is three rubles a skewer; he has only five rubles a day to live on, so he hesitates. A group of truck drivers arrives, who buy up all the *shashlik*. Kostoglotov, miserable, begs them to sell him just a single skewer. They do and he sits there eating, enjoying every morsel.

> He ate thoughtfully as a dog eats after taking his food into a safe corner, and he thought how easy it was to whet human desires and how difficult it was to satisfy them once aroused. For years he had re-garded a hunk of black bread as one of the most precious gifts on earth. A moment ago he had been ready to go and buy some of his breakfast, but then he had smelled . . . the roast meat, the men had given him a skewer to gnaw and already he was be-ginning to feel contempt for bread. [p. 495]

Delighted by the streets, the people, the glass of wine, the *shashlik*, the ice cream he has bought, Kostoglotov is caught up by the queues in front of a department store and swept into the store by the mad rush of buyers. He watches people fighting to buy cardigans and blue soup plates, then observes a man who asks for a shirt both by general size and collar size.

> What was this? There were men rotting in trenches, men being thrown into mass graves, into shallow pits in the perma frost, men being taken into the camps for the first, second and third times, men being jolted from station to station in prison trucks, wearing themselves out with picks, slaving away to be able to buy a patched-up quilt jacket—and here was this neat little man who could remember the size not only of his shirt but of his collar too! [p. 501]

Kostoglotov is abruptly depressed, weighted down by the realization that "he had spent hours buying one vain object after another. . . . Where was it he had traded in his untouched soul of this morning? In the department store . . . No, earlier on, he had drunk it away with that wine. Or even earlier, he had eaten it away with the *shashlik*" (pp. 504–505). If people remember their collar sizes, life is getting too refined; one is being "seduced" by consumerism, by the fleshly comforts of meat and wine, so that the important things, like justice, go by the board.

In order to purify himself, Kostoglotov goes to the zoo. Animals and animal imagery play an important role in *Cancer Ward*. Earlier Solzhenitsyn asks, "But if we stop loving animals, aren't we bound to stop loving humans too?" (p. 273). And those of his characters who have and like animals are good people and affirm life; those who destroy animals are evil. The Kadmins, for example, have two giant dogs to which they are deeply devoted; Dr. Oreshchenkov has a massive St. Bernard, dignified and beautiful, whose tranquillity and "transcendental detachment" are sufficient to make Dontsova forget her cancer pains. But the Kadmins write Kostoglotov that the village council in Ush-Terek hired two hunters to roam the streets, and they shot one of the Kadmins' dogs, Beetle, a dog Kostoglotov loved. "So now they had killed the dog as well," they write. "Why?" (p. 415). (This question is to be picked up later on in the question of the why the man threw the tobacco in the Macaque Rhesus' eyes.) When Zoya goes to a masquerade ball in a monkey costume, some toughs cut off the monkey's tail. This reiterated use of animals, particularly monkeys and dogs, as symbols, prepares the reader for Kostoglotov's culminating experience at the zoo. There he sees the magnificent spiral-horned goat, with "the sort of character a man needed to get through life," and also the caged squirrel on a wheel, "quite oblivious of its tree and the slender branches up above, . . . attracted only by the illusion of sham activity and movement," racing to death at a furious pace and accomplishing nothing. "Here were two meaningful examples, on the right and left of the entrance, two equally possible modes of existence with which the zoo greeted young and old alike" (pp. 506–507): on the one hand the proud loneliness of the goat; on the other, the meaningless work and consumption treadmill of the squirrel.

Kostoglotov hates to see animals in their cages, but he realizes that if he "took their side and had the power, he would still not want to break into the cages and liberate them. This was because, deprived of their home surroundings, they had lost the idea of rational freedom. It would only make things harder for them, suddenly to set them free" (p. 508). Like the squirrel who ignores the lovely tree above for the sham activity of the wheel, men who are caged cannot be freed, because they have lost the habit and context of freedom.

Kostoglotov reaches the empty cage of the Macaque Rhesus, which bears a small plywood sign: "The little monkey that used to live here was blinded because of the senseless cruelty of one of the visitors. An evil man threw tobacco into the Macaque Rhesus's eyes." This fills Kostoglotov with fury. "What went straight to his heart was the childish simplicity with which it was written. This unknown man . . . was not described as 'anti-humanist,' or 'an agent of American imperialism'; all it said was that he was evil. . . . How could this man be simply 'evil'?" Obsessed by that notion of "mindless malignity," Kostoglotov then walks on through the "kingdom of reptiles, vipers and beasts of prey" (p. 509)—the animals who are "by their nature" evil. The monkeys remind him of his fellow political prisoners, but the beasts of prey resemble the camp gangsters, the criminal prisoners, and he concludes, "After all, one can work out who are the guilty ones of this world" (p. 510).

At the railway station, Kostoglotov writes his last letters

to Zoya and Vera, and then sends a postcard to Dyomka describing the zoo and its remarkable animals. He tells the boy how an evil man threw tobacco into the Rhesus monkey's eyes and blinded him, "just like that, for no reason." Kostoglotov then exhorts young Dyomka, who loves truth and literature—and animals: "Get better and live up to your ideals. I'm relying on you" (p. 531). He also sends his regards to Shulubin, the Old Bolshevik who espouses ethical socialism, hoping that he will recover. What Solzhenitsyn is saying is that youth, cut off though it is from ethical socialism by the Stalinist heritage, still retains its idealism and will eventually improve conditions by carrying forward Shulubin's ethical socialism—which is what he means when he has Kostoglotov send his wish for Shulubin's recovery. But even if Shulubin should not survive, his ideas and his words will, as Solzhenitsyn indicates in the Old Bolshevik's last words to Kostoglotov, a quotation from Pushkin: "Not all of me shall die" (p. 485).

Even more than most novelists, Solzhenitsyn lays heavy weight on his final chapters; in these last crucial chapters of *Cancer Ward*, he brings together the private and public strands of the novel. On a personal level, Kostoglotov is moved to relinquish Vera because he is unable to sustain an "idealistic-affectionate" relationship with her, prevented by the "beast in him," the sexual, animal part of his nature. Yet, to save Vera anguish, Kostoglotov does give her up, in a most idealistic and high-minded fashion, because he refuses to permit her to submit to a marriage which would not provide her with all of the consummations a marriage should give—sexual gratification and children included. On the public and political level, Kostoglotov is brought to realize that some men do wrong, not out of antihumanist convictions or because they are American imperialist agents, but simply because they are inherently evil—"the beast in them." They shoot the Kadmins' dog; they cut the tail off Zoya's monkey costume; they throw tobacco into the Macaque Rhesus' eyes and blind it, *just like that*— for no reason other than that they are naturally evil.

Kostoglotov's last public act before leaving for Ush-Terek is also an act of idealism and social responsibility. Though he himself has used his prison cunning to get to the head of the ticket line without waiting, he later keeps one of the camp hoodlums, whom he recognizes, from getting to the front of the queue waiting to board the trains—and so also keeps a group of others from jumping the line who would follow the hoodlum. He could have tried to get to the head of the line himself, with the same kind of cunning, "but the past years had made him tired of such tricks. He wanted things done honestly and in a proper way" (p. 534). Ironically, having restrained himself and the other "evil" people, he finds that those for whom he preserved the queue are black marketeers taking vegetables to Central Asia "to make up for mistakes in the supply system" (p. 533). Kostoglotov finally finds a place for himself on the train and thinks about the trip, aware of how different such travel is from being on a prison transport, and he is for a moment content. He has survived: the war; concentration camp; exile; cancer. Then, suddenly, he is seized with anguish as he remembers:

> An evil man threw tobacco in the Macaque Rhesus's eyes.
> Just like that . . . [p. 536]

And those are the last lines of the novel.

At Solzhenitsyn's September 27, 1967, confrontation with the Writers' Union secretariat, *Cancer Ward* was attacked by a number of writers as "anti-humanitarian," and Solzhenitsyn berated for using the cancer ward as a symbol of society in the Soviet Union. Solzhenitsyn denied both charges.

> Now, as to *Cancer Ward*, I am being criticized for the very title of the story, which is said to deal not with a medical case but with some kind of symbol. I reply that this symbol is indeed harmful, if it can be perceived only by a person who had himself experienced cancer and all the stages of dying. The fact is that the subject [of the book] is specifically and literally cancer, a subject avoided in literature. . . .
> I absolutely do not understand why *Cancer Ward* is accused of being anti-humanitarian. Quite the reverse is true: life conquers death, the past is conquered by the future. . . .
> I am disturbed by the fact that some comrades sim-

ply did not read certain passages of the story attentively, and hence formed the wrong impressions. For example, "twenty-nine [*sic*] [4] weep and one laughs" was a popular concentration-camp saying addressed to the type of person who would try to go to the head of the queue in a mess-hall. Kostoglotov comes out with this saying only so that he may be recognized, that's all. And from this people draw the conclusion that the phrase is supposed to apply to the entire Soviet Union. Or the case of "the Rhesus monkey." She appears twice in the story, and from the comparison it becomes clear that this evil person who throws tobacco in the animal's eyes is meant to represent Stalin specifically. And why the protest over my "just like that"? If "just like that" does not apply, does that mean that this was normal or necessary? [5]

Solzhenitsyn was being less than candid in asserting that the cancer ward was only a literal hospital ward and not a political symbol, although given the circumstances—he was under attack, threatened with expulsion from the Writers' Union and with not having his book published —his lack of candor is understandable. In fact, his remark that the evil man who threw the tobacco in the Macaque's

[4] In his play *The Love-Girl and the Innocent* (p. 34), Solzhenitsyn gives this saying as "*ninety*-nine weep."

[5] *Cancer Ward*, trans. Nicholas Bethell and David Burg (New York: Farrar, Straus & Giroux, 1969), Appendix, pp. 556–557.

eyes was intended specifically to be Stalin in itself indicates the symbolic intentions of the novel.

However, his assertion that in the novel life conquers death, and the future the past is in great measure justified. Both the personal tone and political content—a result, perhaps, of the changes in Moscow, the fall of Malenkov, the replacement of the entire membership of the Supreme Court of the Soviet Union ("All those who'd administered justice for a quarter of a century—gone, at a single stroke" [p. 211])—*are* hopeful. Though he is discharged from the hospital with his tumor reduced, Rusanov—symbolic of the heirs of Stalin—will not live out the year. Podduyev, the Chekist who had himself shot seven members of the Constituent Assembly during the Civil War, is dying, as is the young Stalinist Vadim; their cases are hopeless, their days numbered. Kostoglotov's tumor has been arrested; Dyomka has lost one leg but has survived, his idealism and love of truth intact; and even the Old Bolshevik Shulubin will survive. So, too, of course, another ward patient, the simpleminded Ahmadjan, "one of Beria's boys," survives, after telling how concentration-camp prisoners are fed better than soldiers. "They should give them shit to eat!" he says. "Work? They no work! We take them out to zone, they run off, hide and sleep whole day!" (p. 461). When Kostoglotov asks him if he was joking about feeding human beings shit, Ahmadjan heatedly insists: "I no joke! They no human beings! They no human beings!" (p. 462).

The symbolic identification of cancer ward–prison–

Soviet society is made even more explicit in a scene at the end of the book in which Kostoglotov goes to the *kommendatura* (the police station) to get his papers. He remembers the poor treatment he received earlier and goes full of trepidation, but this time he gets a quite different reception. The Armenian NKVD man there deals with him almost humanely, inquires if he has recovered at the cancer clinic, asks him to sit down—unheard of—and tells him that things are changing, that things will soon be improving for Kostoglotov and those like him. Kostoglotov is genuinely moved, thinks how "a few humane men behind these vile desks and life became completely different," and wonders if this change is temporary or permanent, a matter of a general directive or simply the personal decency of a single individual (p. 522). Whatever it is, he knows the change is long overdue. "A man dies from a tumor, so how can a country survive with growths like labor camps and exiles?" (p. 523). Baruzdin's accusation that Solzhenitsyn intended the end of the novel to lead to the conclusion that "a different [political] road should have been taken [in the USSR]" (Appendix, p. 553) is justified, though his objections to that ending are not. Obviously, Solzhenitsyn's view in *Cancer Ward* is not only that a different course should have been taken in Soviet society, but that, under Khrushchev, a new course was *in fact* begun. How far it would go, or how far it was intended to go, was *not*, in 1955, yet clear.

In an earlier meeting Solzhenitsyn had with the Moscow section of the Writers' Union on November 17, 1966, convened to discuss the first half of *Cancer Ward*, there was general agreement that the novel should be published in the Soviet Union (although this never came to pass), and some of the writers and critics present compared the book to such classics as Leo Tolstoy's *The Death of Ivan Ilyich* and Mikhail Saltykov-Shchedrin's *The Golovlyov Family*. A number of literary-political reservations were expressed too, chief among them whether Solzhenitsyn was depicting all of the Soviet Union as a cancer ward, whether the novel was sufficiently optimistic and life-enhancing, and whether the characterization of Rusanov was successful. Otherwise friendly critics remarked that Rusanov was a caricature, a journalistic creation into whose mouth Solzhenitsyn had failed to breathe life. And it is true that Solzhenitsyn gives his Rusanov no redeeming features; even Rusanov's affection for his wife and children seems no more than an extension of his ambition and self-love.

In reply to his critics, Solzhenitsyn admitted that perhaps he had fallen short in depicting Rusanov. He said that he had tried to show the dogmatic bureaucrat sympathetically, with all his literary resources—well, perhaps not quite with *all*—but that he seemed unable to do so. He knew and agreed with that general literary advice that when you portray good men, show their evil side, and when you depict scoundrels, show their good side; but his trouble came in applying this specifically to Rusanov: constructively, he did not know how to accomplish that without altogether losing the scoundrel in the characterization.

If Solzhenitsyn recognizes and portrays inherent evil, he also portrays inherent virtue. Character after character in the novel is decent, compassionate, and kindly. Dontsova and Gangart are hard-working, dedicated, and honorable physicians, as are their surgical colleagues Lev Leonidovich and Yevgenia Ustinovna. The old Dr. Oreshchenkov is a paragon of gentleness, probity, and concern, as is Dr. Maslennikov, who spends five or more hours of his day writing letters to unknown and nonpaying patients giving them medical advice. Nurses like Olympiada and Zoya do their jobs with sympathy and attention. A patient, Aunt Styofa, is a true Christian, and the orderly, Elizaveta Anatolyevna, is a gentlewoman of impeccable character. Kostoglotov has almost as much difficulty in comprehending the kind of "unpremeditated kindness" and virtue these people exemplify as he does in understanding the evil of the man who blinded the Macaque monkey with tobacco for no reason.

Yet Solzhenitsyn is not primarily interested in dealing with subtle ambiguities of character. His good people are good and easily identifiable as virtuous, and his evil people as wicked; and most of his characters' actions are equally unambiguous. This is not because Solzhenitsyn is simple or lacks insight into the complexity of human motives and behavior—no such lack is evidenced in *The First Circle*, for example—or sensitivity to nuances of character and action. On the contrary, he seems deliberately to be choosing moral and psychological simplicity as he de-

liberately chooses elemental environments in human life—
the camps, the *sharashka*, the cancer ward—where choices
must be relatively unambiguous. As he calls for a stripped-
down, almost ascetic life, a life which resists the blandish-
ments of possessions, place, and power, so he calls for a
stripped-down evaluation of action and character. Do I
betray my neighbor, colleague, or parent? Very well, then,
that is evil. Do I bear false witness in order to convict a
man and get his apartment? Criminal. Do I collaborate
with the forces of repression and terror? Appalling. Just
as in *One Day in the Life of Ivan Denisovich*, Solzhenitsyn is attempting to see beyond complexity and ambiguity
to an organic wholeness and goodness upon which human
personal and social happiness can be built.

A number of the obsessions with which Solzhenitsyn
is saddled continue to be reiterated. The primary one, of
course, is his hatred for injustice, his detestation of the
political police, the "state within a state" that the KGB is,
and of the camps which it peoples with its victims. That
special compassion he maintains for underdogs—for prisoners, for minority nationalities, for women, for exiles, for
the halt and the lame—is everywhere evident. In the
"Grand Hotel" setting of the *Cancer Ward*, Solzhenitsyn
is able to show the same broad section of Soviet life that
he was able to in the similar settings of the penal colony
and the research institute. There are young and old, men
and women, Communists and non-Communists, Uzbeks,
Kazakhs, Tatars, Germans, Russians—and all have in one

way or another been involved with or touched by the purges, the KGB, and the camps.

> But a hard life improves the vision. There were some in the wing who immediately recognized each other for what they were. Although in no way distinguished by uniform, shoulder insignia or armband, they could still recognize each other easily. It was as if they bore some luminous sign on their foreheads, or stigmata on their feet and palms. . . . The Uzbeks and the Kara-Kalpaks had no difficulty in recognizing their own people in the clinic, nor did those who had once lived in the shadow of barbed wire. [p. 478]

Solzhenitsyn's obsession with literature and its role in Russian life is also apparent throughout the novel, directly and in constant literary references—from Leo Tolstoy to Ernest Hemingway [6]—and literary asides. The Chekist Yefrem Podduyev is, finally, brought to a reconsideration of his entire life by reading Leo Tolstoy's *What Men Live By* and learning that men live by love. (Solzhenitsyn mocks Rusanov in this connection, and by implication all the heirs of Stalin, by having Rusanov ask Podduyev about the book, but be unable to understand its message because he thinks the author is Alexei Tolstoy, and he "only wrote optimistic and patriotic works, otherwise he wouldn't have been printed. . . . And, let me tell you, he won the Stalin Prize three times!"—p. 108.) Solzhenitsyn damns

[6] Kostoglotov's "emasculation" owes a literary debt to Jake Barnes's in Ernest Hemingway's *The Sun Also Rises*.

contemporary Soviet literature in an observation made by the youth Dyomka, who "was rather frightened at the thought of how many writers there were. In the last century there had been about ten, all of them great. In this century there were thousands. . . . No one could have time to read all their books, and when you did read one, it was as if you might just as well not have done. Completely unknown writers floated to the surface, won Stalin prizes, then sank back forever. Nearly every book of any size got a prize the year after it appeared. Forty or fifty prizes popped up every year" (p. 122). Early in the novel Solzhenitsyn has Dyomka reading a two-year-old issue of *Novy mir*. In it is the Vladimir Pomerantsev essay, "On Sincerity in Literature," which was one of the first works in the first (1953) "thaw." When Rusanov's daughter, Alla, comes to visit her father in the ward and describes to him in the most crass and opportunistic terms the literary life in Moscow, Dyomka summons up enough courage to ask her shyly about Pomerantsev's thesis that there must be sincerity in literature. In the most patronizing and cliché-ridden "socialist-realist" terms, Alla thereupon "explains" to him:

> Sincerity can't be the chief criterion for judging a book. If an author expresses incorrect ideas or alien attitudes, the fact that he's sincere about them merely increases the harm the work does. Sincerity becomes *harmful*. Subjective sincerity can militate against a truthful presentation of life. . . .

. . . Telling the people the truth doesn't mean telling them the bad things, harping on our shortcomings. On the other hand, one may describe the good things quite fearlessly, so as to make them even better. Where does this false demand for so-called harsh truth come from? Why does truth suddenly have to be harsh? Why can't it be radiant, uplifting, optimistic? Our literature ought to be wholly festive. When you think about it, it's an insult to people to write gloomily about their life. They want life to be decorated and embellished. [pp. 288–289]

Though Dyomka maintains, "Literature is the teacher of life," the geologist Vadim insists, "Literature is to divert us when we're in a bad mood," and he bristles at the thought that writers are any cleverer than "practical workers" (p. 289). Rusanov's daughter goes on to add:

Describing something that exists is much easier than describing something that doesn't exist, even though you know it's going to exist. What we see today with the unaided human eye is not necessarily the truth. The truth is what we *must* be, what is going to happen tomorrow. Our wonderful tomorrow is what writers ought to be describing today. [p. 290]

Solzhenitsyn is obviously contemptuous of positive, optimistic, and literarily embellished books. The kind of literature he approves of and is concerned with is revealed in a

talk between Kostoglotov and the ward orderly, Elizaveta
Anatolyevna, one of the most moving character por-
trayals in the novel. Kostoglotov asks her why she reads
only French books, and she replies, "They don't hurt you
so much" (p. 479), commenting further:

I have no idea whether these Frenchmen were
keeping silent about more important things, or whether
the same kind of cruel life as ours was going on outside the world of their books. . . .

. . . I know of no books closer to our life that
wouldn't irritate me. Some of them take the readers
for fools. Others tell no lies; our writers take great
pride in that achievement. They conduct deep research
into what country lane a great poet traveled along in
the year 1800 and something, or what lady he was referring to on page so-and-so. It may not have been an
easy task working all that out, but it was safe, oh yes,
it was safe. They chose the easy path! But they
ignored those who are alive and suffering today. . . .

These literary tragedies are just laughable compared with the ones we live through. . . .

Children write essays in school about the unhappy,
tragic, doomed, and I-don't-know-what-else life of
Anna Karenina. But was Anna really unhappy? She
chose passion and she paid for her passion—that's
happiness! She was a free, proud human being. But
what if during peacetime a lot of greatcoats and
peaked caps burst into the house where you were
born and live, and order the whole family to leave

house and town in twenty-four hours, with only what
your feeble hands can carry?

... So why should I read *Anna Karenina* again?
Maybe it's enough—what I've experienced. Where
can people read about us? *Us?* Only in a hundred
years' time? [pp. 481–482]

It is precisely this task that Solzhenitsyn, like no other
Soviet writer, has taken as his responsibility and his burden: to write about what his generation, his people, and
his country have experienced, to write about the Soviet
Us here and now and not wait for someone to write about
it in a hundred years' time, and to write about all of it
truthfully, out of his own experience, vision, and love of
country. In *Cancer Ward* he succeeds in conveying a
considerable portion of that experience: the 1935 purge in
Leningrad in which a quarter of the population of the
city was deported; the failure of Soviet leaders to prepare
for World War II and the siege of Leningrad; class and
ethnic prejudices and Great Russian chauvinism; consumer
and housing shortages and the lack of many of the simplest
amenities of life while rockets and atomic bombs are being
developed. Most important of all, he shows the shadow
of the KGB over everyone and everything—the cruel and
arbitrary state within the state, with its purges of individuals
and whole classes and peoples, with its interrogations,
prisons, camps, exiles, and execution, with its omnipresent
informing, denouncing, and terror. Solzhenitsyn depicts
both individual human beings and the entire population

continually threatened by poverty, terror, and war. In *Cancer Ward* the hospital is a state where a man's life is at stake, just as it is in Ivan Denisovich's concentration camp and in Gleb Nerzhin's *sharashka*. Like the prisoners and the exiles, the patient is an outcast, a "criminal" who is a prisoner, not only of fate, but of the hospital, the doctors, and the science of medicine, just as the citizens of the Soviet Union are the prisoners, not only of fate, but of the state, the heirs of Stalin and the KGB, and the government of "scientific socialism." Just as he portrays the terrible sense of individual impotence in the face of disease, so too, explicitly and by implication, Solzhenitsyn delineates the same sense of social and individual impotence in the face of the KGB and the Soviet system. What ray of hope there is lies in the belief that the ice is breaking up in the thaw of Khrushchev's de-Stalinization, his restoration of "socialist legality," reorganization of the judiciary and the government, and downgrading of the powers of the political police. In 1955, when the action of the novel takes place, light could be dimly seen or imagined at the end of the tunnel, but since 1964 that light has grown dimmer and the tunnel longer and more labyrinthine.

5 ⚡ One Life in
the Soviet Day

> Justice has been the common patrimony of humanity
> throughout the ages. It does not cease to exist for the
> majority even when it is twisted in some ("exclusive")
> circles.
>
> *Aleksandr Solzhenitsyn*

In Russia open political debate has almost never been
allowed to become a part of the national life, and as a
result literature has often become the substitute for a
political forum. This has laid a very heavy burden on
Russian writers and writing, and has simultaneously made
both the targets of every regime which has ruled the
country. Such a concern for the "word" has been especially true of the Soviet rulers, who, after Stalin came to
power, saw to it that almost every original, critical, or
individual voice was silenced. For purposes of their own,
the heirs of Stalin believed that more freedom could be
allowed to writers and intellectuals; but the notion that in
doing so only the Kremlin's purposes would be served
was a serious miscalculation that grew quite naturally out
of Soviet circumstances, for the prevailing assumption was

that writers and intellectuals were instruments of the Party and the state, to be used by the Kremlin in the ways it thought necessary. Had not even Stalin himself allowed considerable latitude to the writers during the "Great Fatherland War" when circumstances warranted, and had he not swiftly and effectively stifled their voices immediately thereafter when he thought it in his interest? Both the Khrushchev and the Brezhnev-Kosygin governments attempted to impose their own orthodoxies on the writers and intellectuals without employing outright Stalinist methods, but gradually, after 1964, and on a number of occasions even before then, restraints on literary and intellectual freedom grew so restrictive that they could, reasonably, only be called neo-Stalinist.

In that moment of thaw in which he allowed the publication of *One Day in the Life of Ivan Denisovich*, Khrushchev opened a veritable Pandora's box politically for the heirs of Stalin, but he also released a burgeoning, if faint, ray of hope for many ordinary people and for most of the intelligentsia that the areas of freedom and nonconformity would be considerably broadened. After all, this was the first book to deal with the *camp*, that central institution of Soviet life, which, like the censorship, was omnipresent but never publicly acknowledged. In the happenstance of choosing Solzhenitsyn to publish, the Soviet rulers had met a man of very singular character and courage with whom they were going to have much more trouble than they had with such other critical writers as Pasternak, Vladimir Dudintsev, or Ehrenburg. Like their tyrannical progenitor, the heirs of Stalin had long dealt with writers and intellectuals with the edged contempt and blunt bludgeon that most practical and powerful men of affairs reserve for artists, writers, and intellectuals in a country where Party and government have brought almost every writer to heel or silenced him. As a result, they were unprepared for the tenacity, integrity, and bravery of this middle-aged man who refused to knuckle under, who refused to be bought off, who persisted in telling the truth as he saw it, who despite their strictures bore witness to what his country and his people had suffered, to what he himself had seen and endured, for all his people and all the world to read about. Perhaps the heirs of Stalin underestimated him: perhaps they thought that a man who had been through the war, prison, concentration camp, exile, and cancer ward could not muster such resources; but those experiences, to use a favorite Soviet literary cliché, had tempered the man's steel. Certainly they might have killed him, as they had killed many others, and they might still; but after the publication of *Ivan Denisovich* with Khrushchev's personal imprimatur, the authorities, impeded by their desire to disavow at least some aspects of Stalin's methods, found it increasingly difficult. With the publication of Solzhenitsyn's other novels abroad and the award of the Nobel Prize, executing him became even more complicated, and even outright persecution beyond the pernicious harassments the KGB could so skillfully inflict became more pregnant with serious consequences, political and intellectual, domestic and foreign.

One Life in the Soviet Day

Because Solzhenitsyn's writings are so deeply rooted in his life and in the life around him, their verisimilitude has special persuasiveness and impact. Such "critical realism," though in some measure a literary flaw, was undoubtedly politically forceful and made his writings far more dangerous to the heirs of Stalin than the eccentric or fantastic works of such men as Pasternak, Andrei Sinyavsky, and Yuli Daniel, or of those who wrote in elliptical or Aesopian language of the realities of Soviet life. For the first time in the history of the Soviet state a novelist was writing without the usual hypocrisy, illusions, delusions, and self-censorship most Soviet writers had consciously or otherwise saddled themselves with in depicting Russian life. In Solzhenitsyn's works the injustices of Stalinism are delineated and documented with a specificity, candor, and emotional force that refuse to call them "aberrations" or "distortions," but steadily insist on their criminality and on their perpetrators as criminals. The novels do not simply blame Beria or Abakumov or Ryumin, or even Stalin alone; in essence, they indict the whole Soviet system and a good portion of the Soviet people as well for complicity and cooperation in Stalinist terror and tyranny.

In his novels and to a lesser extent in his life, Solzhenitsyn encompassed the historic experience of his generation and of the country. Although his writings are specifically set in time between World War II ("The Incident at Krechetovka Station" takes place in 1943) to the early Khrushchev era (*Cancer Ward* takes place in 1955), Solzhenitsyn deals with almost all the major upheavals and traumas of some five decades of Soviet history following the Bolshevik Revolution: the Civil War, the NEP, collectivization, the murder of Sergey Kirov, the Great Purges, the Spanish Civil War, the Hitler-Stalin Pact, the war with Finland, Russia's unpreparedness in the face of the Nazi invasion, World War II, the exile and expulsion of whole peoples—Crimean Tatars, Volga Germans, Chechen-Ingush, Balkars, and so forth—the military failures and ineptitudes during the war, the Zhdanov repressions after the war, the Doctors' Plot, the death of Stalin, and the realities of life under the heirs of Stalin. Moreover, in all his writing, it is apparent that Solzhenitsyn is dealing with Soviet reality *now, today*—with the same institutions afflicting the people and the country, with the same elite group composed of much the same individuals controlling the institutions, with the old injustices not yet rectified, and with new ones still being inflicted. Solzhenitsyn, then, is not addressing himself merely to wartime realites or immediate postwar conditions, but to the *present-day* life of his country and his people.

Solzhenitsyn's work and person have become a symbol and focus of the conflict between the heirs of Stalin and the small group of political and literary dissidents. One element in that conflict was exposed in Solzhenitsyn's public assault on censorship and government control of publication. Solzhenitsyn's demands that government censorship be discontinued, that the Union of Writers become an organization to defend writers *against* the state instead of a bureaucratic arm of the regime, that there be absolute freedom for publication of belles-lettres are symbolic of the urge for freedom, not only in the arts and in science, but in many other areas of society. (Members of other institutions of Soviet life—factory managers, union leaders, local and regional political leaders—have also sought increasing autonomy; and although there have been grudging concessions from the central authorities in various "decentralization" schemes, there has been relatively little delegation of power from the "center.") The Kremlin is not prepared to consider, nor does it seem ever to have been prepared to consider, granting such concessions in the arts during any of the thaws which have occasionally softened the rigors of Soviet literary life. In addition, it has never been willing to surrender the close centralized control of the entire nation in all its parts which might, by extrapolation, be called for in Solzhenitsyn's proposals about censorship and the Writers' Union.

Solzhenitsyn's work is also a powerful attack on the Soviet system *from inside.* Clearly no Marxist-Leninist, nor greatly impressed with the record of the Soviet regime, Solzhenitsyn is, like his creation Shulubin, an "ethical socialist," and therefore constantly calls into question the morality of the Soviet leaders and their institutions, high and low. The stress is on *ethical* rather than *socialist:* Solzhenitsyn's views are basically moral rather than political, except insofar as ethics are ancillary to politics. More obsessed by the problems of man's evil and goodness—exemplified in the man who throws tobacco in the Macaque's eyes and wantonly blinds it, as well as in Matryona's saintliness and Spiridon's considered virtue— than he is by the political ramifications of those ethical considerations, Solzhenitsyn cannot uncover the roots of evil or of goodness by tracing them to the social system and its production and class relations, by employing the orthodox and vulgar Marxist analysis of base and super-structure.

There is no deep-rooted Russian tradition of and love for personal freedom, but there is a profound commit-ment to "justice"; from this commitment Solzhenitsyn truly speaks for his people. Andrei Amalrik may be right in maintaining that for most Russians "freedom" is syn-onymous with "disorder," that "personal" and "individual" human personality has no particular value and must be considered insignificant and therefore subordinate to the "communal" interest. He may even be right in contending that Russian love of justice is far less vigorous than Russian respect for brute force, and that, in practice, what passes for love of justice is simply a kind of equalitarianism which says, "Nobody should live better than I do."

> This idea of justice is motivated by hatred of every-thing outstanding, which we [Russians] make no ef-fort to imitate, but, on the contrary, try to bring down to our level, by hatred of any sense of initiative, of any higher or more dynamic way of life than the life we live ourselves. This psychology is, of course, most typical of the peasantry and least typical of

the "middle class." However, peasants and those of peasant origin constitute the overwhelming majority of our country.[1]

But Solzhenitsyn disagrees, and is convinced that his stubborn insistence on justice may find more fertile ground in the Russian spirit than his equally stubborn concern for freedom and the individual personality, for Solzhenitsyn believes the urge to justice is inherent in the spirit of all men everywhere.

Justice has been the common patrimony of humanity throughout the ages. It does not cease to exist for the majority even when it is twisted in some ("exclusive") circles. Obviously it is a concept which is inherent in man, since it cannot be traced to any other source. Justice exists even if there are only a few individuals who recognize it as such. The love of justice seems to me to be a different sentiment from the love of people (or at least the two coincide only partially). And in periods of mass decadence, when the question is posed, "Why bother? What are the sacrifices for?" it is possible to answer with certainty: "For justice." There is nothing relative about justice, as there is nothing relative about conscience. Indeed, justice *is* conscience, not a personal conscience but the conscience of the whole of humanity. Those who clearly recognize the voice of their own con-

[1] *Will the Soviet Union Survive until 1984?* (New York: Harper & Row, 1970), p. 35.

science usually also recognize the voice of justice. I consider that in all social or historical questions (if we are aware of them, not from hearsay or books, but are touched by them spiritually), justice will always suggest a way to act (or judge) which will not conflict with our conscience.[2]

But Solzhenitsyn, and the remainder of that courageous band of dissidents and reformers in the Soviet Union, *are* living in a period and a society of mass decadence, and despite their moral courage and intrepidity, their prospects are surely bleak. Their numbers are small, their power is extremely limited, and they are trapped between the Scylla of a hostile regime and the Charybdis of a hostile or indifferent populace.

In spite of all this, Solzhenitsyn, like Faulkner, is a curious kind of "optimist": he sincerely believes that man will not only endure, he will prevail. Though his short stories all end pessimistically, all the novels end on a note of contingent but positive optimism: Ivan Denisovich manages to survive another day, almost a happy day, and hopes that he will manage to survive the rest of his prison term; Gleb Nerzhin deliberately has himself sent from the first circle of hell to its lowest depths, consciously heartened and hardened by his determination to survive and to write his history, which will indict the institutions and individuals responsible for having brought him and his

[2] "Two from Solzhenitsyn," *Dissent*, Nov.–Dec. 1970, p. 558. This is part of a letter written to a group of students who had visited Solzhenitsyn.

country to such a pass; and Oleg Kostoglotov finds that his body and the body politic have had simultaneous remissions from the cancers that afflict them, and though he returns to exile, he knows that it is no longer perpetual exile, and he has the hope that things are on the mend. Throughout, Solzhenitsyn's hopefulness is guarded, made ambiguous by irony and humor, sometimes even by gallows humor, but the hope is there, strong and pulsing, refusing to quit, refusing to die; and in this courageous assertion of hope his life and his work fuse. A Yugoslav critic, Sveto Maslesa, has sensitively explained why the man and his work have come to be of such symbolic importance—and not only in the Soviet Union.

> Solzhenitsyn has done more than could be expected from a mortal man: he has offered his own life as the last pawn to his human faith. Thus, his personal tragedy has become a part of his literary vision. This is the point at which his writing and his life have joined hands. This is why we have asserted that one cannot discuss Solzhenitsyn's books as a literary phenomenon only. His literary work, born as the offspring of his personal tragedy, is nothing but the way in which the author is engaged in a concrete social and ideological situation. . . . Within the framework of that society, he decided to state his views and to implement them. Solzhenitsyn has even turned his literary work into action. It is our duty to greet and sup-

port such an artist, such a man, regardless of the part of the world from which his voice is heard.[3]

Solzhenitsyn, then, has borne witness to the tragedy of the Soviet people and the Soviet writer; his life and his work are testimony to both and give us a deeper, fuller, more compassionate understanding of what they have endured. Solzhenitsyn has dared to see the emperor naked and to speak out. He has had the courage and character to be what he made his character Matryona:

> . . . the righteous one without whom . . . no village can stand.
> Nor any city,
> Nor our whole land.[4]

He stands with that group of Soviet saints and martyrs, dissidents and dissenters, who have stood against the juggernaut. In their ideals and courage, in their intelligence and persistence is the only leaven from which a new and better society can arise where now the "archipelago of Gulag" stretches over one-sixth of the earth.

[3] Solzhenitsyn: Unity of Literature and Life," *Odjek* (Sarajevo), No. 21–22 (Nov. 1970).
[4] "Matryona's House," in *"We Never Make Mistakes": Two Short Novels*, trans. Paul W. Blackstock (Columbia: University of South Carolina Press, 1963), p. 100.

⚡ Bibliography

There is no comprehensive bibliography of Solzhenitsyn's works or of the works about him. The most extensive one to date, published on November 24, 1969, in Munich by the Radio Liberty Library, is entitled *A. I. Solzhenitsyn (A Bibliography)*, and contains published and unpublished works as well as some of the many translations of Solzhenitsyn's works into other languages.

The Russian émigré publisher Possev Verlag has published a multivolume edition of Solzhenitsyn's writings in Russian, *Piesy, rasskazy, stati* (Frankfort on the Main, 1969).

WORKS BY SOLZHENITSYN

Cancer Ward. Translated by Nicholas Bethell and David Burg. New York: Farrar, Straus & Giroux, 1969.

Cancer Ward. Translated by Rebecca Frank. New York: Dial Press, 1968.

"Candle in the Wind," *Grani*, March 1969.

"City on the Neva," *New York Times*, December 10, 1970.

"Easter Procession," translated by Manya Harari, *Time,* March 21, 1969.

The First Circle. Translated by Michael Guybon. London: Harvill, 1968.

The First Circle. Translated by Thomas P. Whitney. New York: Harper & Row, 1968.

"Flamme au vent (où La lumière qui est en toi)," *Politique Hebdo,* October 15, 1970.

For the Good of the Cause. Translated by David Floyd and Max Hayward. New York: Praeger, 1964.

"An Incident at Krechetovka Station." Translated by Paul W. Blackstock. In *"We Never Make Mistakes": Two Short Novels.* Columbia: University of South Carolina Press, 1963.

"The Incident at Krechetovka Station." Translated by Andrew R. MacAndrew. In *Great Russian Short Novels.* New York: Bantam Books, 1969.

The Love-Girl and the Innocent. Translated by Nicholas Bethell and David Burg. New York: Farrar, Straus & Giroux, 1969.

"Matryona's Home," translated by H. T. Willett, *Encounter,* May 1963. Also in *Half-Way to the Moon,* edited by Patricia Blake and Max Hayward. London: Weidenfeld & Nicholson, 1964.

"Matryona's House." Translated by Paul W. Blackstock. In *"We Never Make Mistakes": Two Short Novels.* Columbia: University of South Carolina Press, 1963.

One Day in the Life of Ivan Denisovich. Translated by Max Hayward and Ronald Hingley. New York: Praeger, 1963.

One Day in the Life of Ivan Denisovich. Translated by Ralph

Parker. Introduction by Marvin Kalb. Foreword by Alexander Tvardovsky. New York: Dutton, 1963.

"Prose Etudes and Short Stories," translated by H. T. Willett, *Encounter*, March 1965.

"Prose Poems," *New Leader*, January 18, 1965.

"Prussian Nights," *Die Zeit*, November 1969.

"The Right Hand," *Atlantic Monthly*, May 1969.

"Two from Solzhenitsyn," *Dissent*, November–December 1970.

"Zakhar the Pouch." In *For Freedom: Theirs and Ours*, edited by R. G. Davis-Poynter. New York: Stein and Day, 1969. (This Solzhenitsyn sketch was published anonymously, the author's name, the translator's name, and the source deliberately withheld.)

WORKS ABOUT SOLZHENITSYN

Anonymous. "A. Solzhenitsyn i dukovnaia missiva pisatelia," *Grani*, No. 64 and No. 65, 1967.

——. "The Faces of Solzhenitsyn," *London Observer*, August 30, 1970.

——. "One Black Day in the Life of Alexander Solzhenitsyn," *Economist*, November 15, 1969.

——. "A Prize and a Dilemma," *Time*, October 19, 1970.

——. "Remission from Fear," *Time*, November 8, 1968.

——. "Solzhenitsyn," *Liberal Expressen*, No. 11, 1969.

——. "Solzhenitsyn: A Candle in the Wind," *Time*, March 23, 1970.

——. "Soviet Mud-slinging," (*Manchester*) *Guardian Weekly*, December 20, 1969.

——. *Tra toritarismo e sfruttamento: Interventi di A. I. Solzhenitsyn*. Milan: Jaca Books. 1968.

———. "The Writer as Russia's Conscience," *Time*, September 27, 1968.

———. "Writer in the Eye of the Storm," *Economist*, October 26, 1970.

Ashanin, Charles. "An Open Letter to the Union of Soviet Writers," *Christian Century*, December 17, 1969.

Barnes, Clive. "Solzhenitsyn 'Play,'" *New York Times*, October 18, 1970.

Bethell, Nicholas. "Solzhenitsyn Can Still Write—He Just Can't Publish," *New York Times Magazine*, April 12, 1970.

Blake Patricia. "A Diseased Body Politic," *New York Times Book Review*, October 27, 1968.

———. "New Voices in Russian Writing," *Encounter*, April 1963.

Blumenfeld, F. Yorick. "Another Pasternak?" *Newsweek*, July 29, 1968.

Bonavia, D. "Russia's Demand to Be Free," *London Times*, November 15, 1969.

Brown, D. "*Cancer Ward* and *The First Circle*," *Slavic Review*, June 1969.

Chamberlin, William H. "Stalin's Death Camps as Seen from Inside," *Wall Street Journal*, February 21, 1963.

Cook, Bruce. "Two Novels by Mr. Solzhenitsyn Prove Even Saints Can Be Dull," *National Observer*, December 30, 1968.

Crankshaw, Edward. "Solzhenitsyn's 'Easter Spirit,'" *Toronto Mail and Globe*, April 8, 1969.

———. "Voice the Kremlin Wants to Silence," *London Observer*, April 6, 1969.

Fainsod, Merle. "Among Many Stalinist Days, One in Particular," *Herald Tribune Books*, April 7, 1963.

Fanger, Donald. "Solzhenitsyn: Ring of Truth," *The Nation*, October 7, 1968.

Bibliography

Foote, Timothy. "A Nobel Prize Winner Who Deserved It," *Life*, October 23, 1970.

Friedberg, Maurice. "Gallery of Comrades Embattled Abed," *Saturday Review*, November 9, 1968.

Frioux, Claude. "Soljénitsyne: Le Prophète et son pays," *Politique Hebdo*, October 15–21, 1970.

Gaev, A. "Telling the Grim Truth," *Bulletin of the Institute for the Study of the USSR*, April 1963. (Hereafter referred to as *Bulletin*.)

———. Writers and Critics in the USSR," *Bulletin*, June 1968.

Galambos, Lajos. "I Protest," *Kortars*, March 1963.

Hegge, Per Egil. "A Telephone Call to Solzhenitsyn," *Atlas*, December 1970.

Hingley, Ronald. "A New Voice out of Siberia," *Sunday Times* (London), December 2, 1962.

Ingold, F. P. "Die Auseinandersetzungen um Solschenizyns 'Krebsstation' in der Sowetunion," *Neue Zürcher Zeitung*, July 20, 1968.

Jacob, A. "Alexandre Soljénitsyne a rejeté les arguments de ses accusateurs," *Le Monde*, November 12, 1968.

Jacobson, Dan. "The Example of Solzhenitsyn," *Commentary*, May 1969.

Juhasz, Maria. "The Heroism of the Anti-Hero," *Kortars*, May, June 1969.

Kalem, T. E. "The Invisible Nation," *Time*, November 2, 1970.

Kerr, Walter. "Solzhenitsyn's Vision of Man's Adaptability," *New York Times Theater Section*, October 25, 1970.

Korn, K. "Opfer des Systems, Ueberwindung des Systems," *Frankfurter Allgemeine Zeitung*, November 12, 1968.

Lask, Thomas. "As the Clock Nears Midnight," *New York Times*, February 28, 1969.

———. "The Bars Are Never Visible," *New York Times*, September 11, 1968.

Levy, David. "Politics of Soviet Literature," *Montreal Star*, November 28, 1969.

Licko, Pavel. "One Day with Alexander Isaevich Solzhenitsyn," *Kulturny Zivot*, March 31, 1967.

———. "One Day with Solzhenitsyn—An Interview," *Soviet Survey*, July 1967.

Littell, Robert. "Solzhenitsyn's *Cancer Ward*," *Newsweek*, March 17, 1969.

Louis, Victor. "Solzhenitsyn Lives Martyr's Role," *Washington Post*, March 16, 1969.

Lukacs, Gyorgy. "About Literature and Marxist Action," *Literarni noviny*, March 1964.

———. "Contemporary Socialist Reality," *Neue Rundschau*, No. 3, 1964. Reprinted in *Kritika*, March 1965.

———. "Soljénitsyne," *Politique Hebdo*, October 15–21, 1970.

———. "Solzhenitsyn and Contemporary Socialist Reality," *Kritika*, March 1965.

Marin, Yuri. "Soviet Writers in the Struggle for Intellectual Freedom," *Bulletin*, April 1969.

Mark, Elisabeth. "La Littérature soviétique en tutelle," *Politique Hebdo*, October 15–21, 1970.

Mihajlov, Mihajlo. "The Artist as the Enemy," *New York Times*, October 24, 1970.

———. "Dostoyevsky's and Solzhenitsyn's House of the Dead," *Bulletin*, August 1965. (This essay was subsequently included in *Russian Themes*).

———. *Russian Themes*. New York: Farrar, Straus & Giroux, 1968.

Monas, Sidney. "Ehrenburg's Life, Solzhenitsyn's Day," *Hudson Review*, Spring 1963.

Bibliography

Morris, Bernard. "What a Red Prisoner Lived For," *Washington Post*, January 27, 1963.

Pismo, George. "The Exclusion of Alexander Solzhenitsyn from the Writers' Union," *Bulletin*, February 1970.

Pomerantsev, K. "Mysli o Solzhenitsyne," *Russkaia mysl*, December 12, 1968.

Pritchett, V. S. "Hell on Earth," *New York Review of Books*, December 19, 1968.

Rothberg, Abraham. "Aleksandr Solzhenitsyn: The Obsession of Morality," *Interplay*, February 1971.

——. "One Day; Four Decades," *Southwest Review*, Spring 1971.

——. "Squaring the Circle," *Interplay*, April 1969.

Saikowski, Charlotte. "A Nobel Solution for Solzhenitsyn," *Christian Science Monitor*, December 2, 1970.

——. "Solzhenitsyn: The Kremlin Still Hunts a Way Out," *Christian Science Monitor*, October 23, 1970.

Salisbury, Harrison. "The World as a Prison," *New York Times Book Review*, September 15, 1968.

Slonim, Marc. "Solzhenitsyn," *New York Times Book Review*, November 8, 1970.

Snyder, Louis. "Solzhenitsyn Play a First in Minneapolis," *Christian Science Monitor*, October 14, 1970.

Ssachno, H. "Finale im Fall Solschenizyn?" *Suddeutsche Zeitung*, November 14, 1969.

Stevens, Edmund. "Solzhenitsyn Collecting the Nobel Prize," *Newark Evening News*, November 4, 1970.

Weidlé, Wladimir. "Russkoe kultornoe nasledie," *Vozdushnie Puti*, No. 5, 1967.

Young, Scott. "Admiration for a Brilliant Russian Who Writes History as Literature," *Toronto Mail and Globe*, February 4, 1969.

Zavalishin, V. "Solzhenitsyn, Dostoevsky, and Leshenkov-Klychkov," *Bulletin*, November 1963.

Zorza, Victor. "The Right to Write," (*Manchester*) *Guardian Weekly*, October 17, 1970.

Index

Index

Aleksandr Solzhenitsyn:
The Major Novels

Designed by R. E. Rosenbaum.
Composed by Vail-Ballou Press, Inc.,
in 11 point linotype Janson, three points leaded,
with display lines in monotype Deepdene.
Printed letterpress from type by Vail-Ballou Press
on Warren's 1854 Text, 60 pound basis,
with the Cornell University Press watermark.
Bound by Vail-Ballou Press
in Interlaken ALP book cloth
and stamped in All Purpose foil.
Endpapers are Strathmore Grandee Spanish Gold.